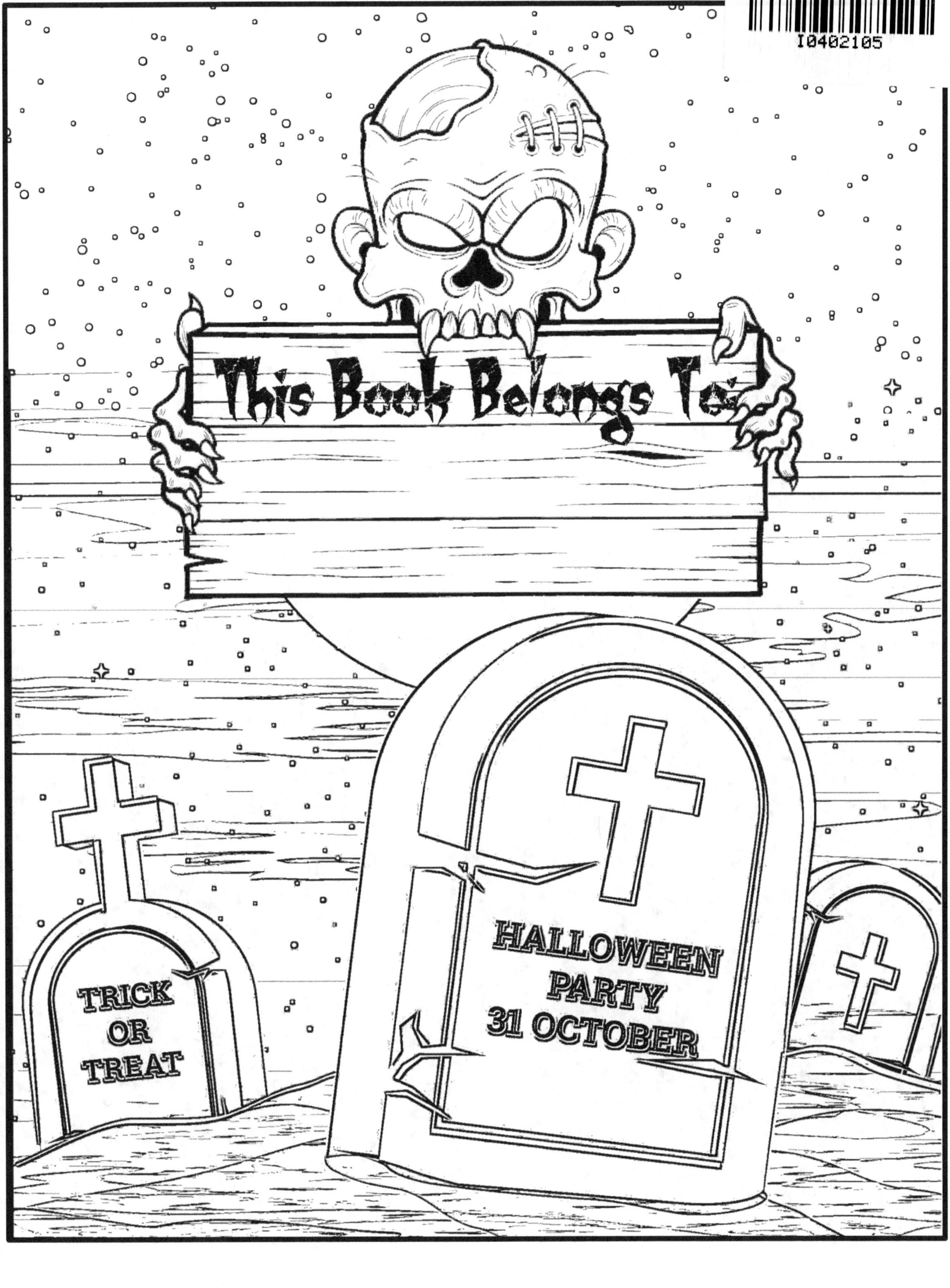
This Book Belongs To:
TRICK
OR
TREAT
HALLOWEEN
PARTY
31 OCTOBER

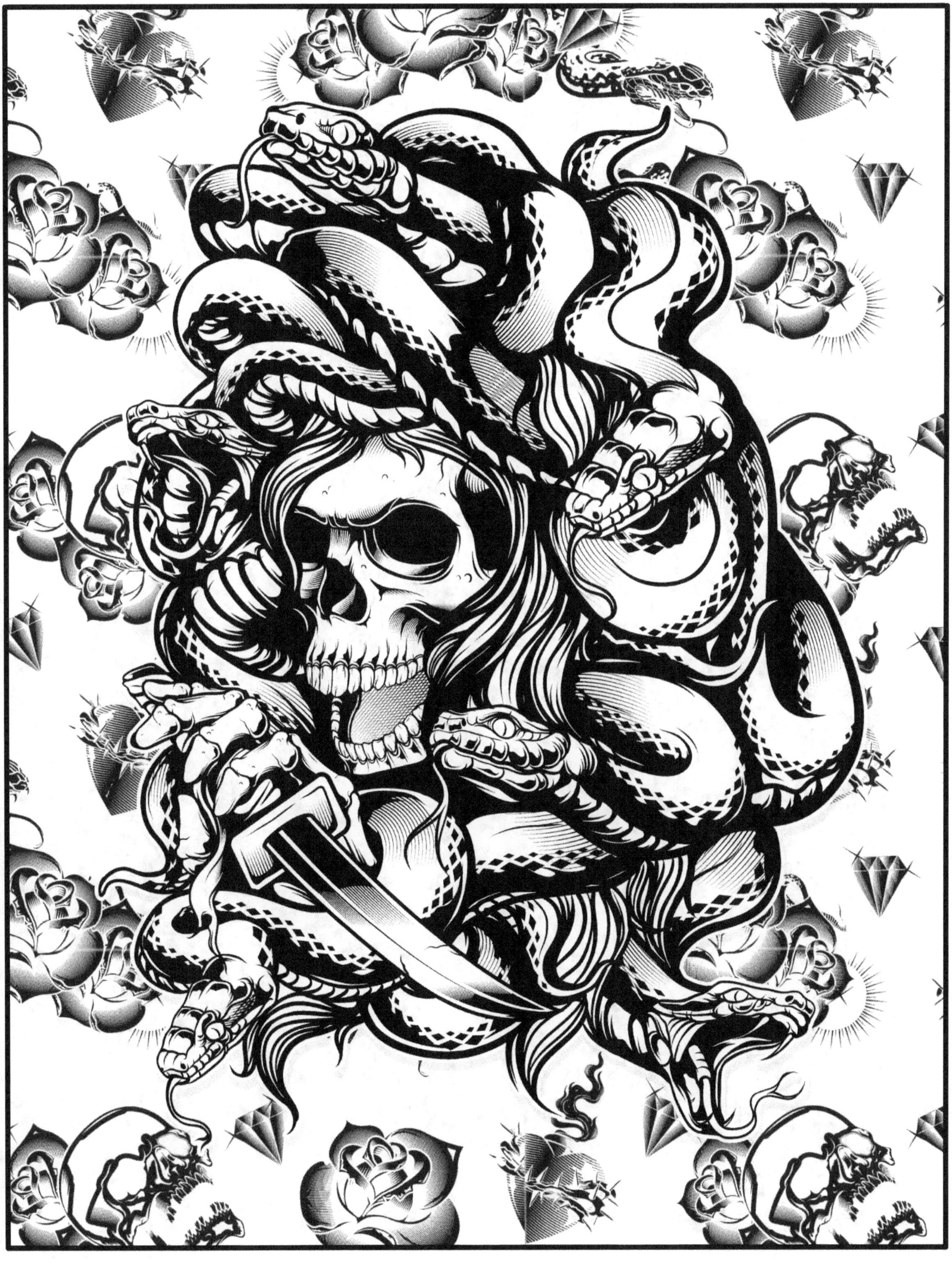

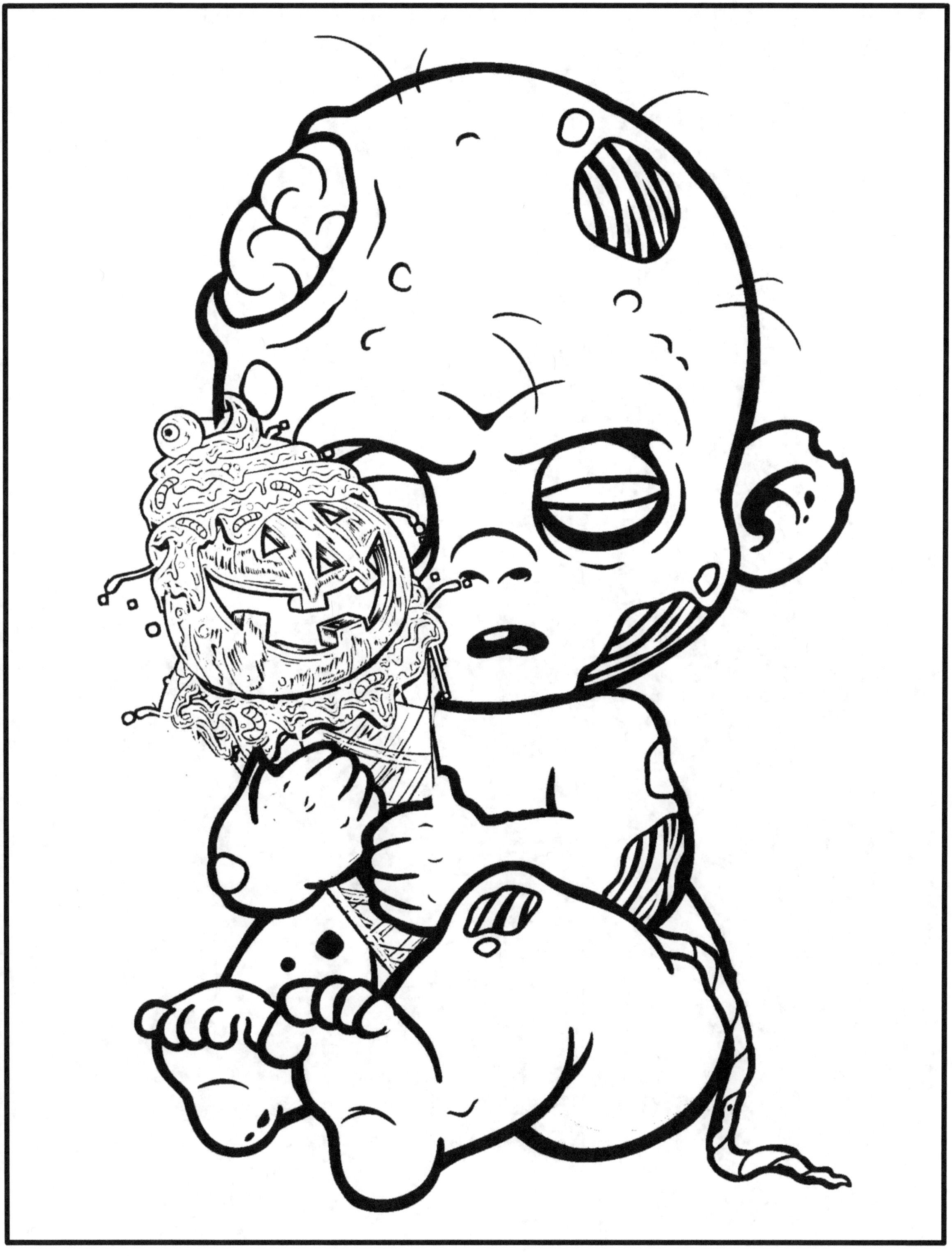

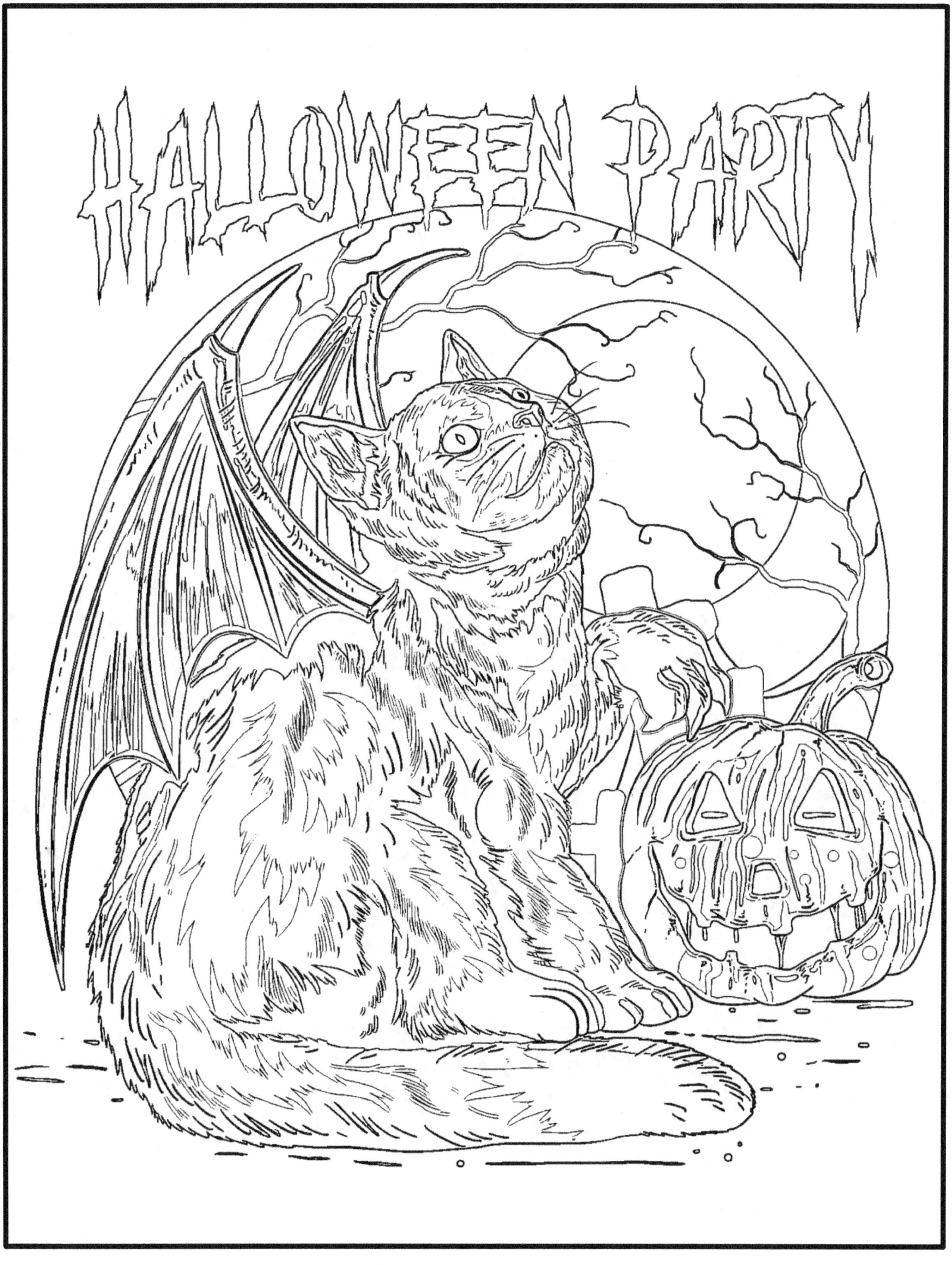
HALLOWEEN PARTY

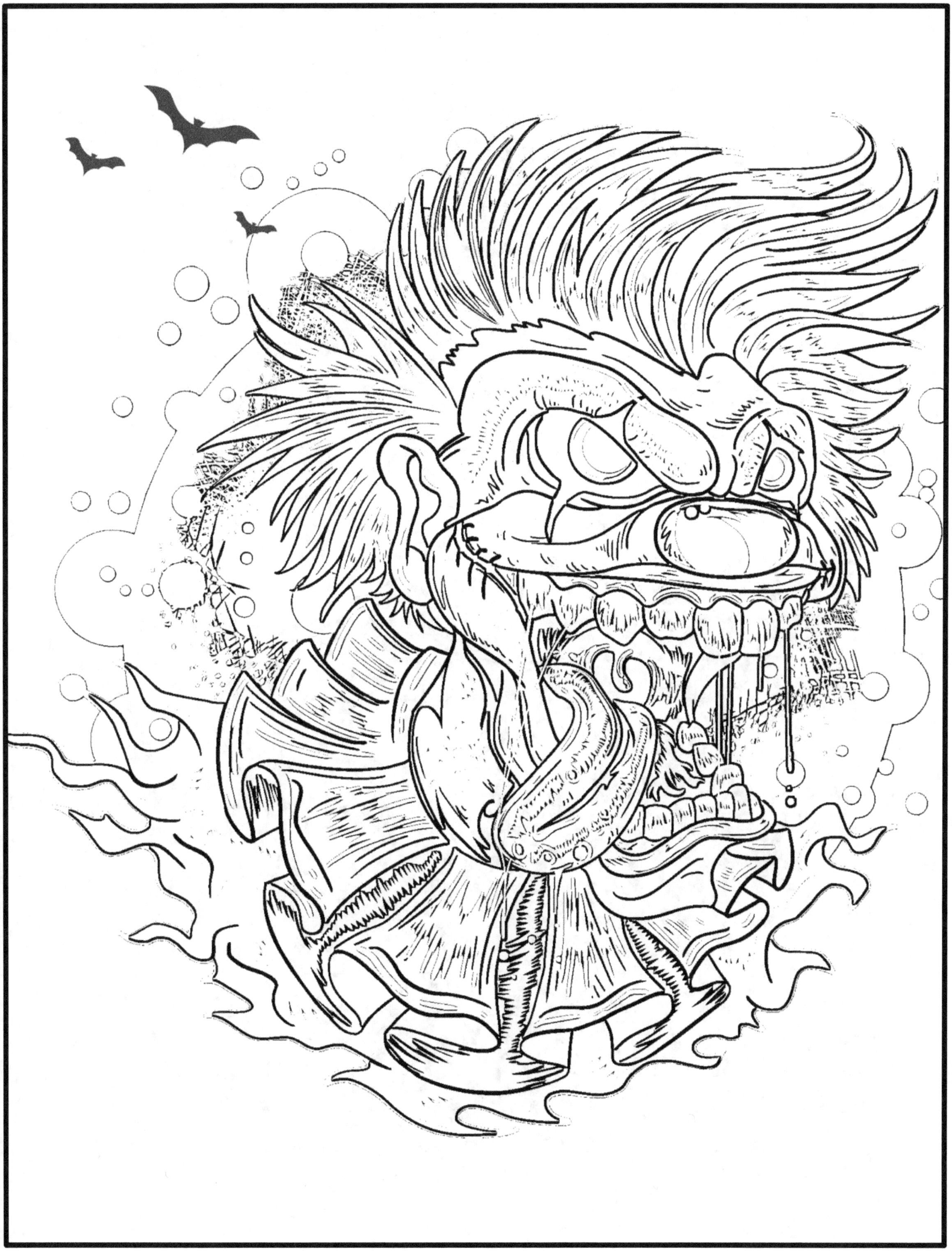

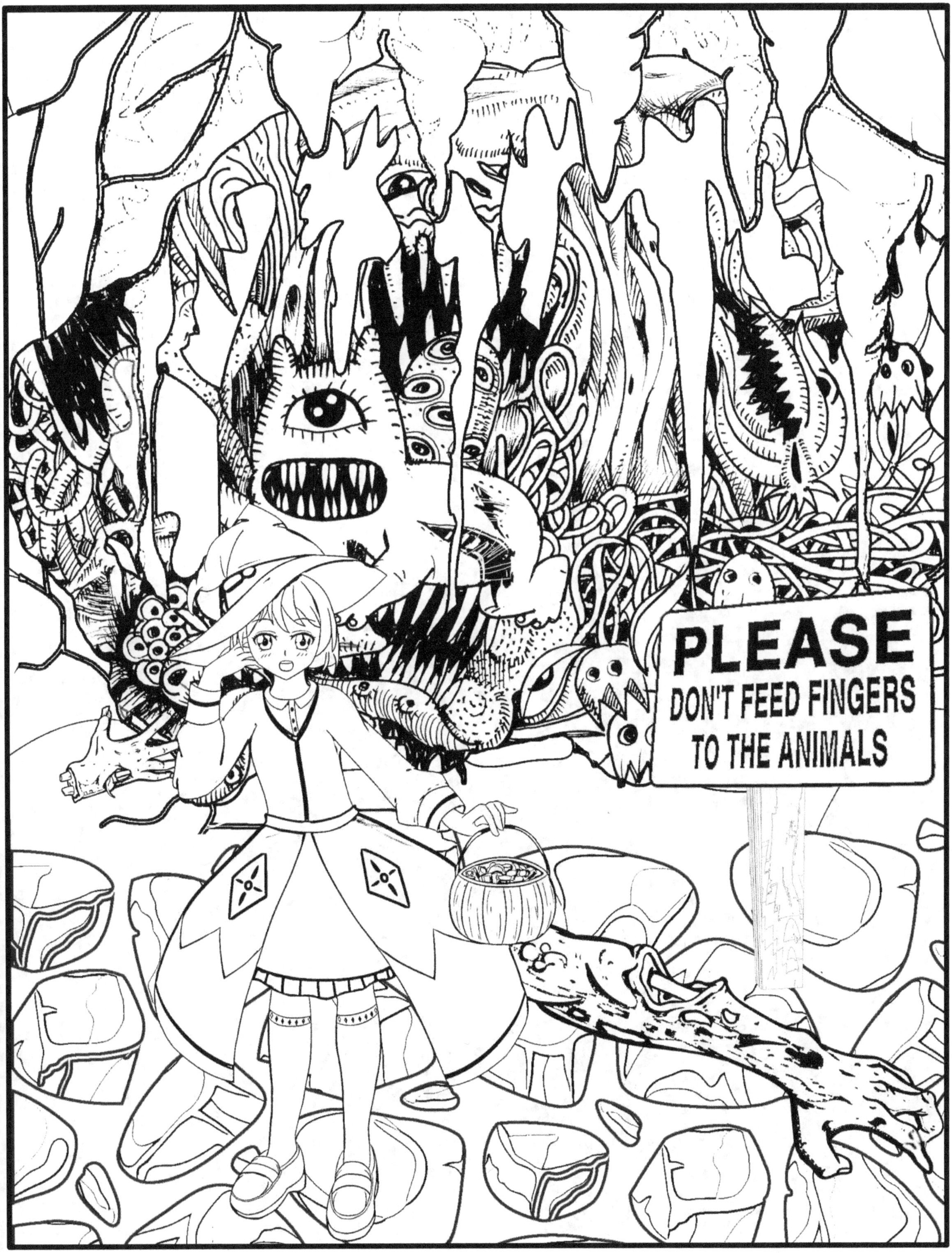
PLEASE
DON'T FEED FINGERS
TO THE ANIMALS

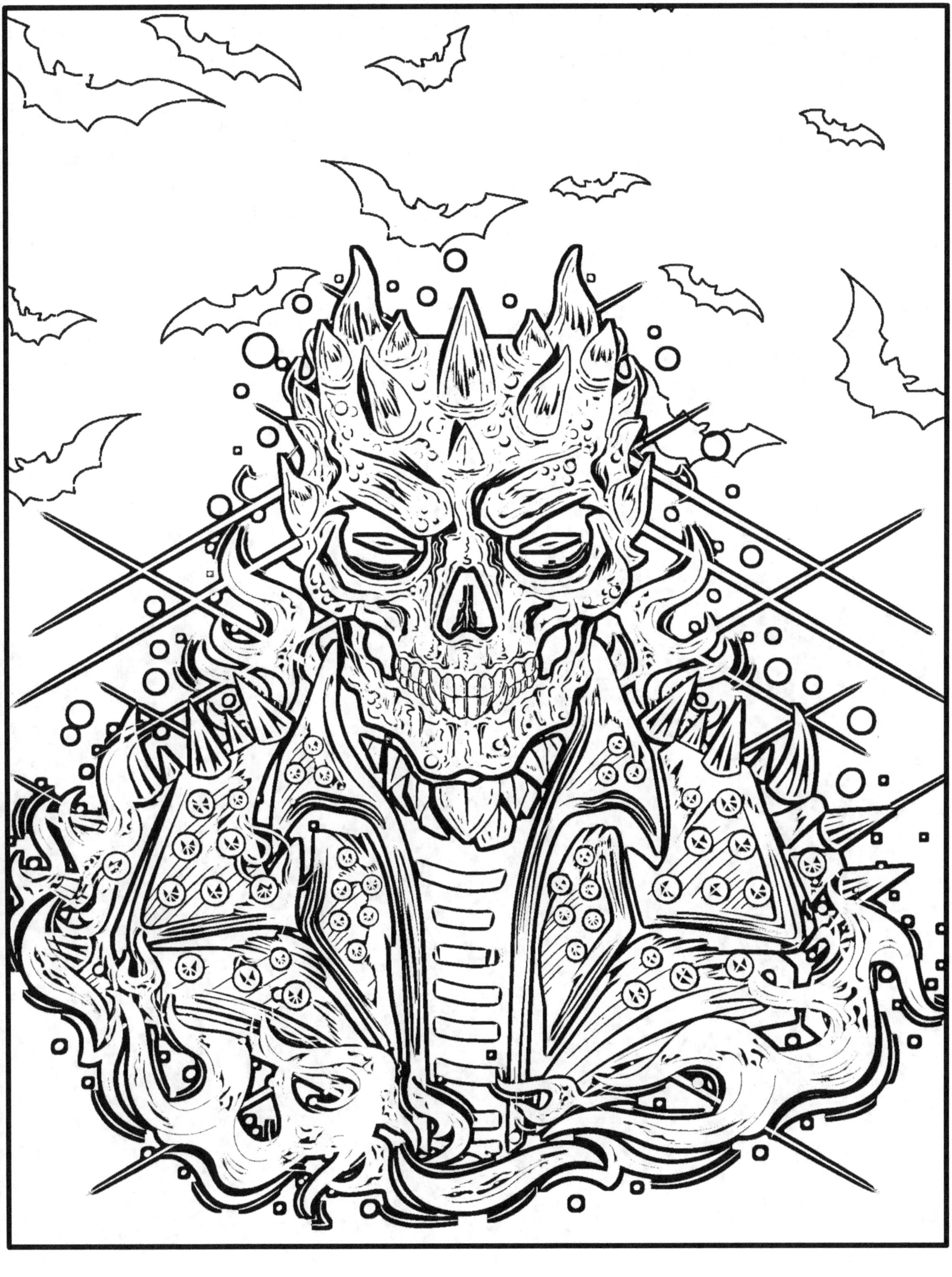

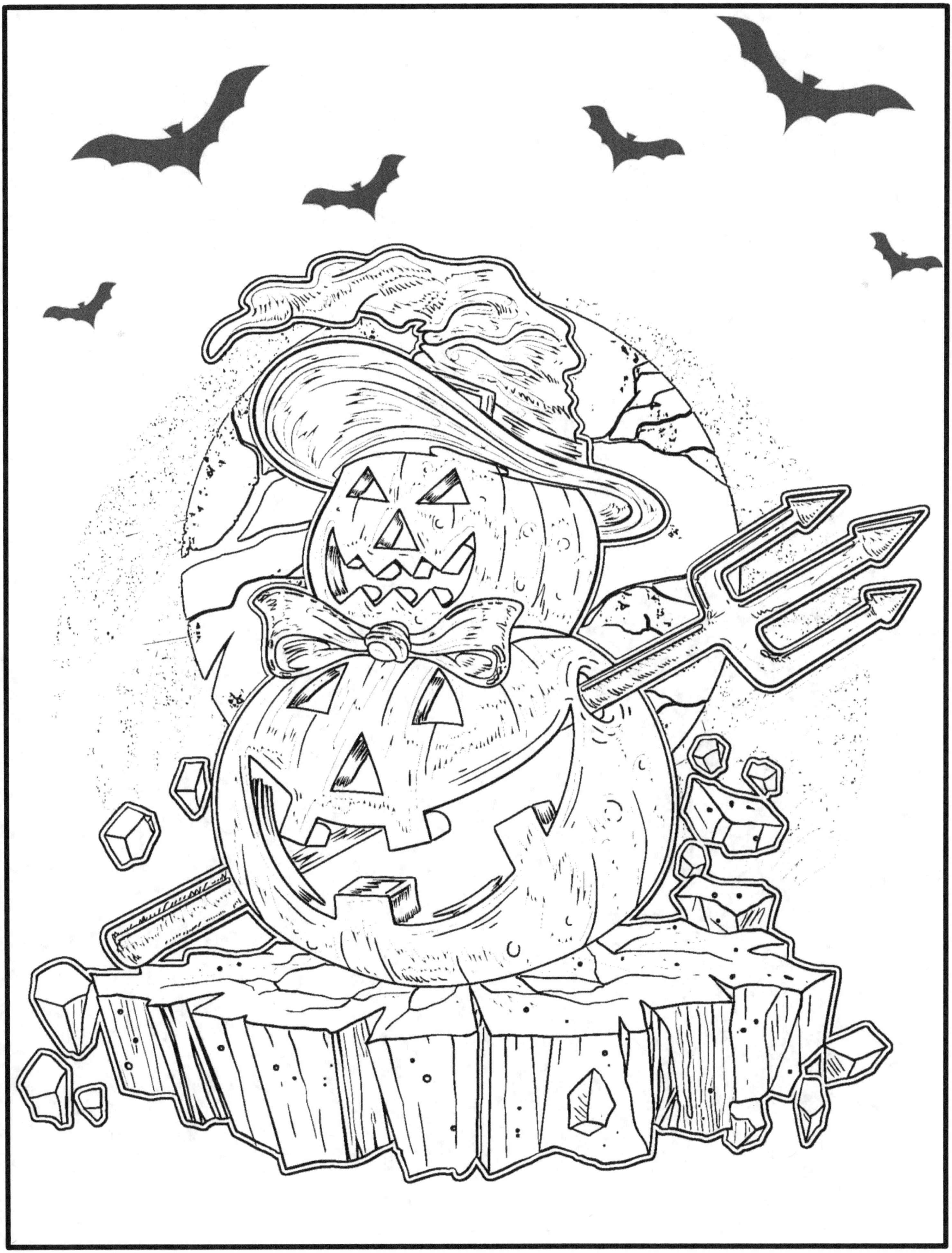

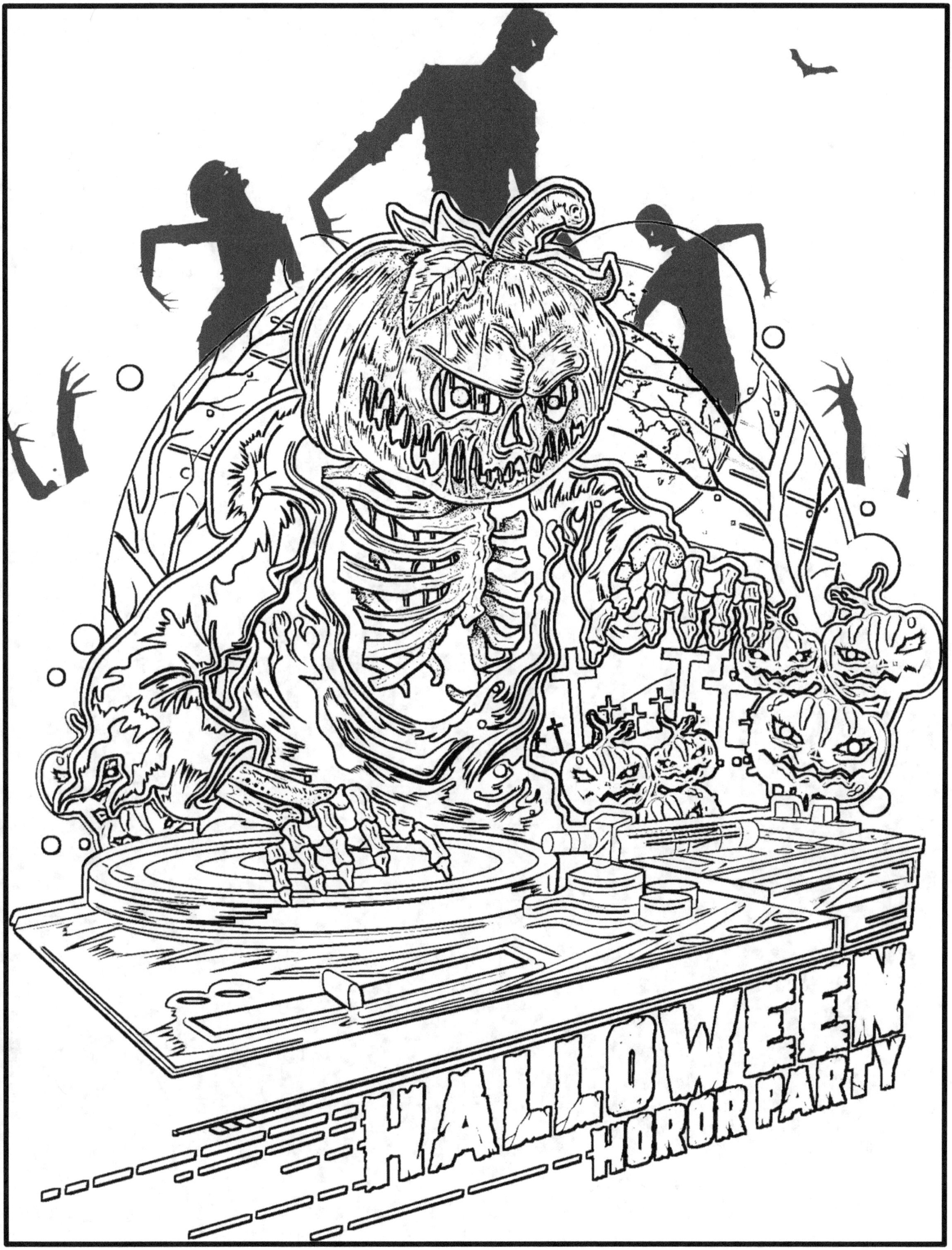
HALLOWEEN
HOROR PARTY

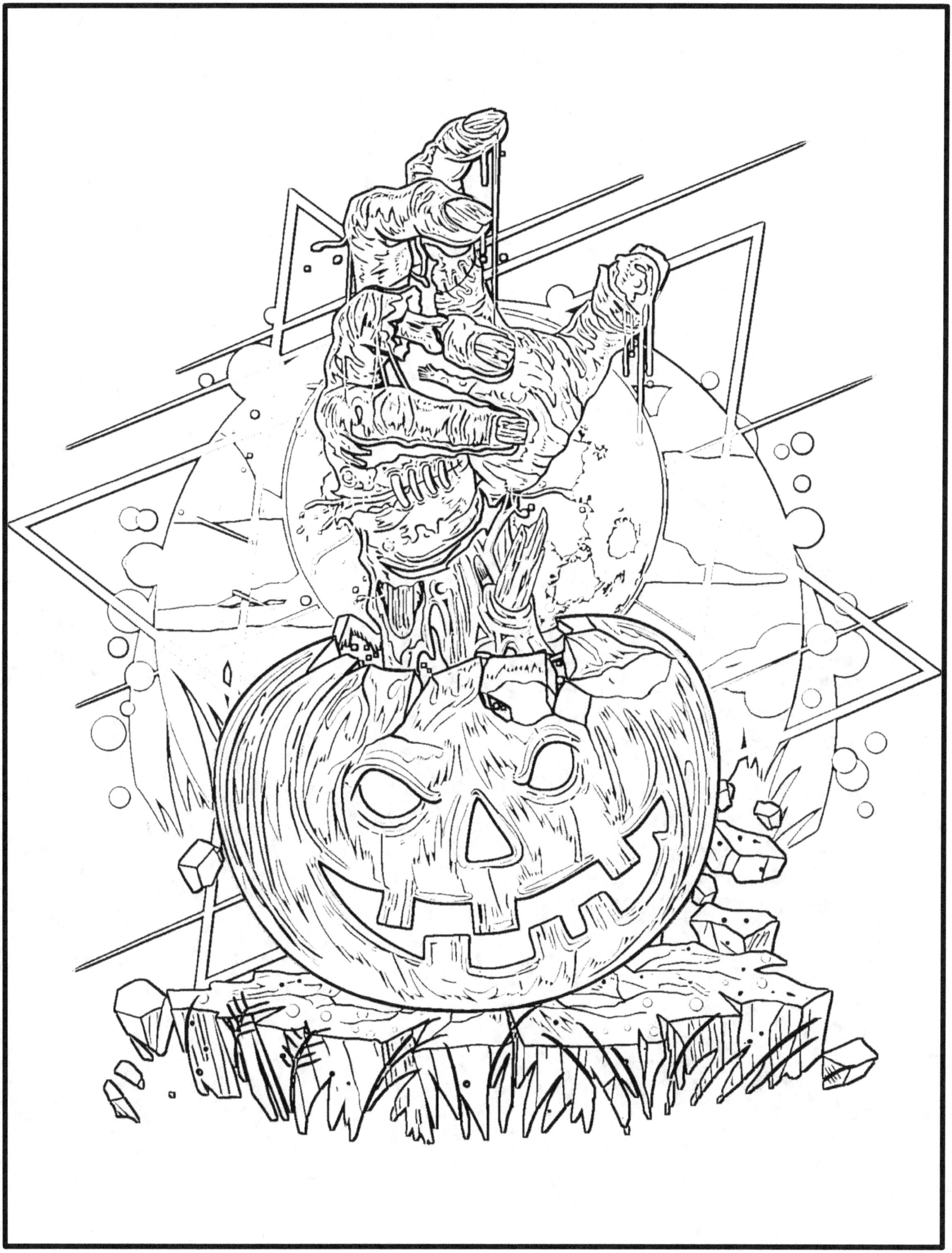

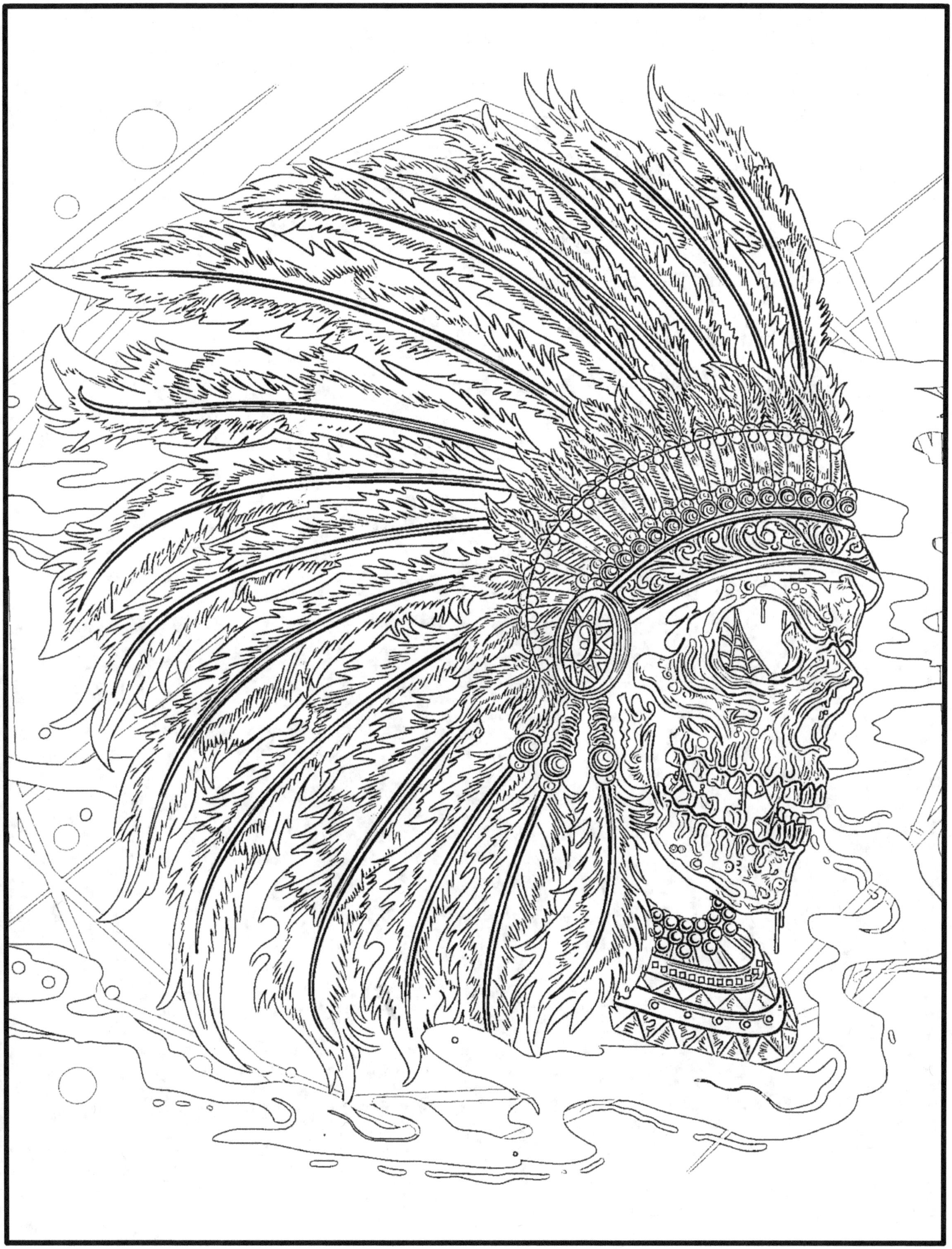

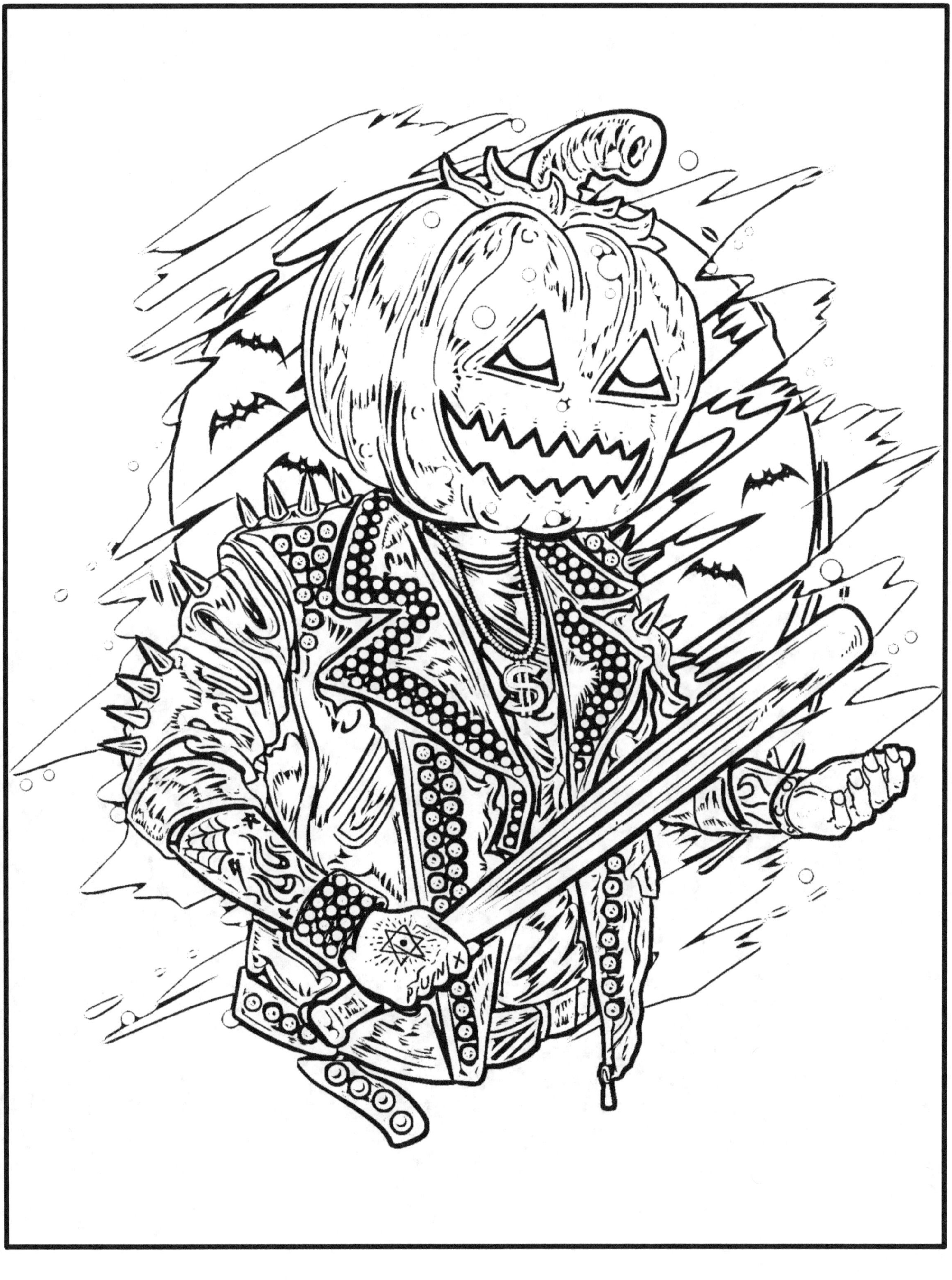
PUNX

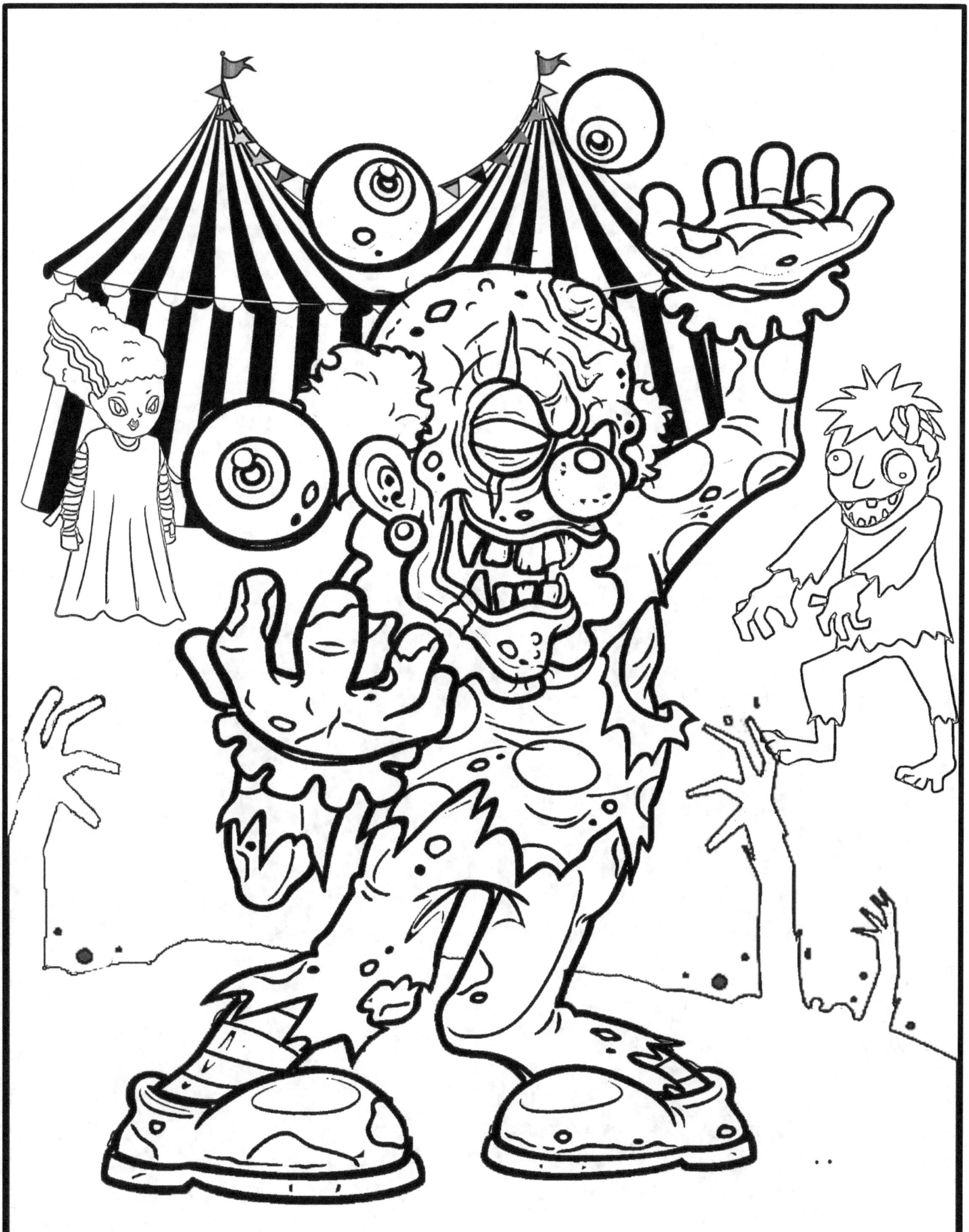

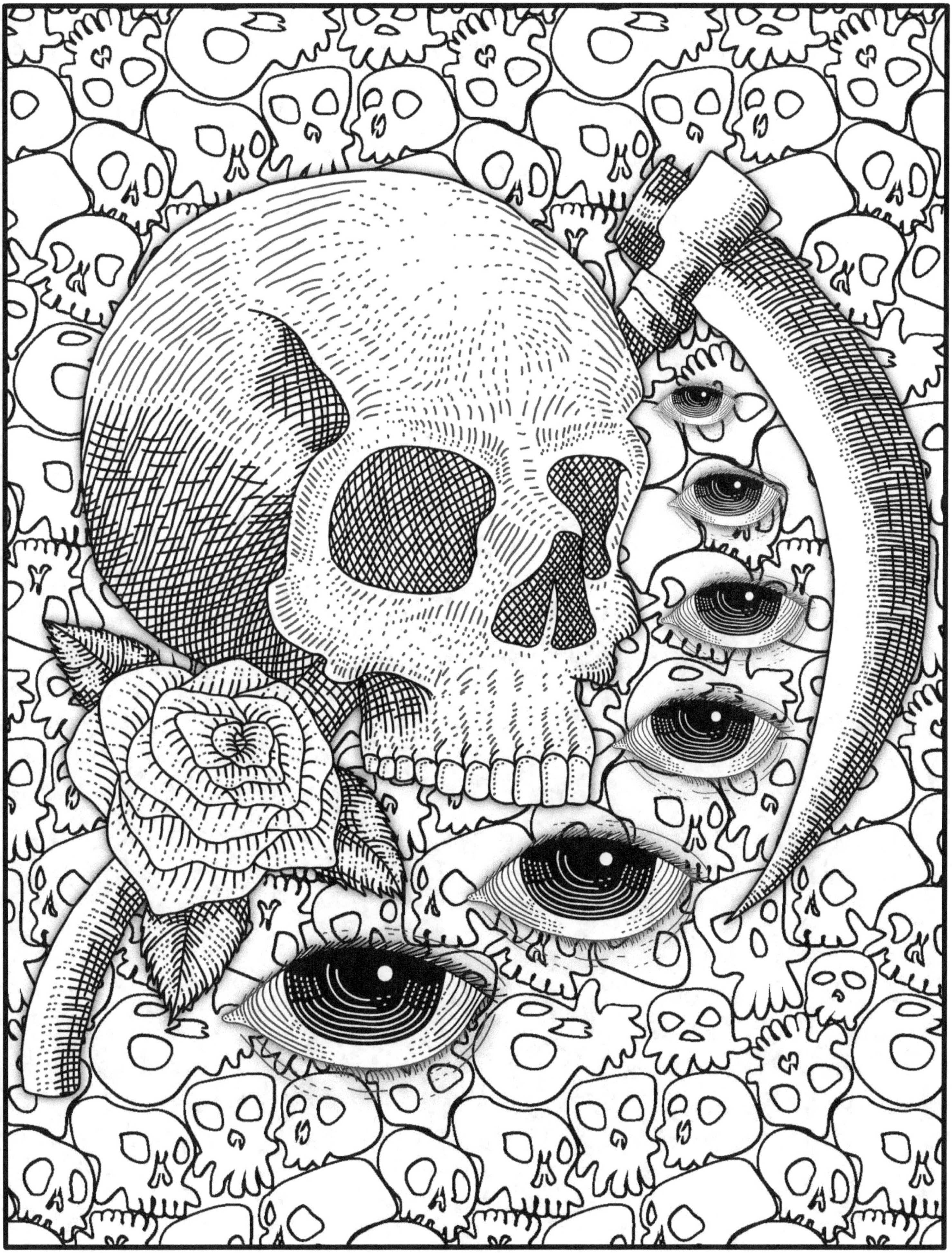

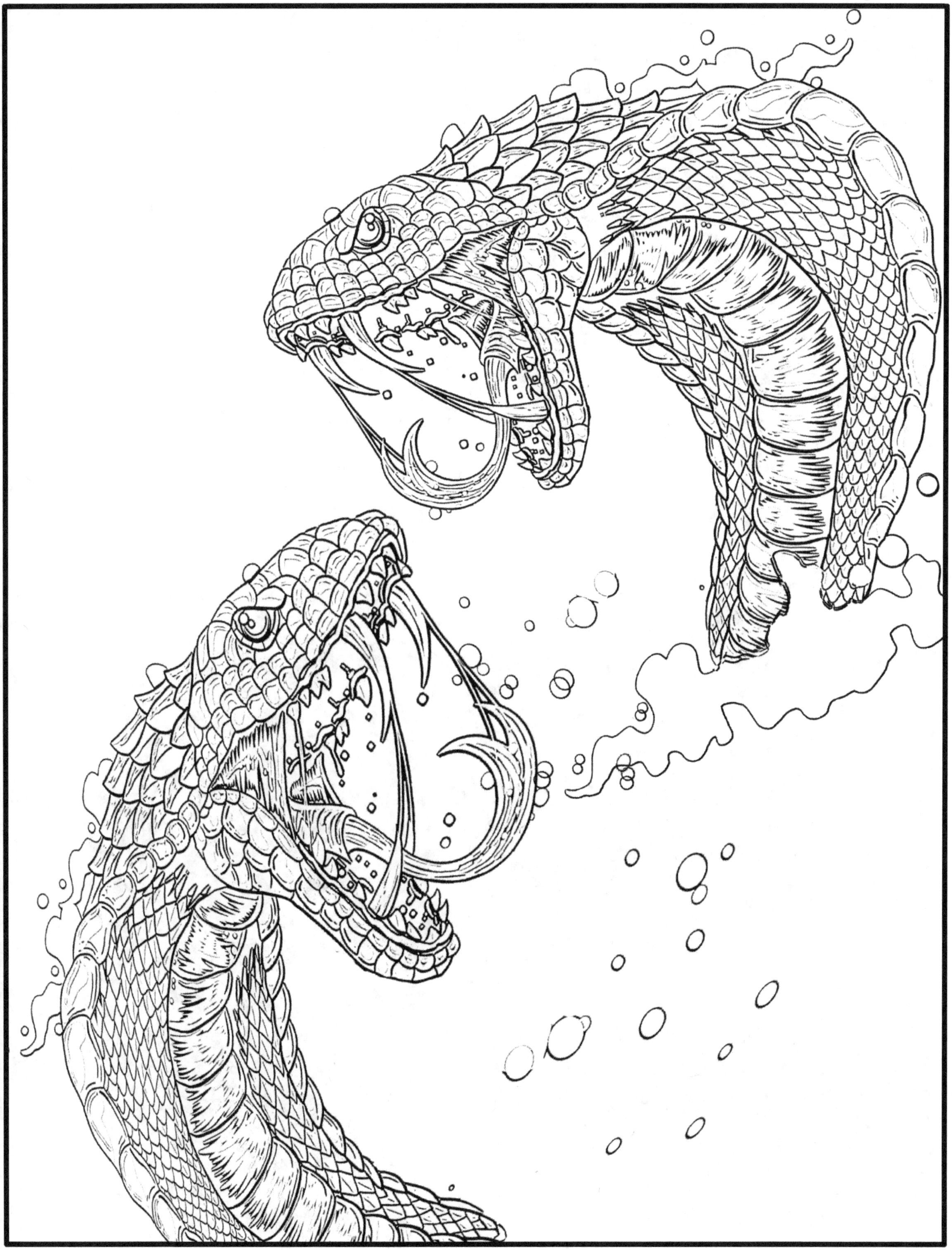

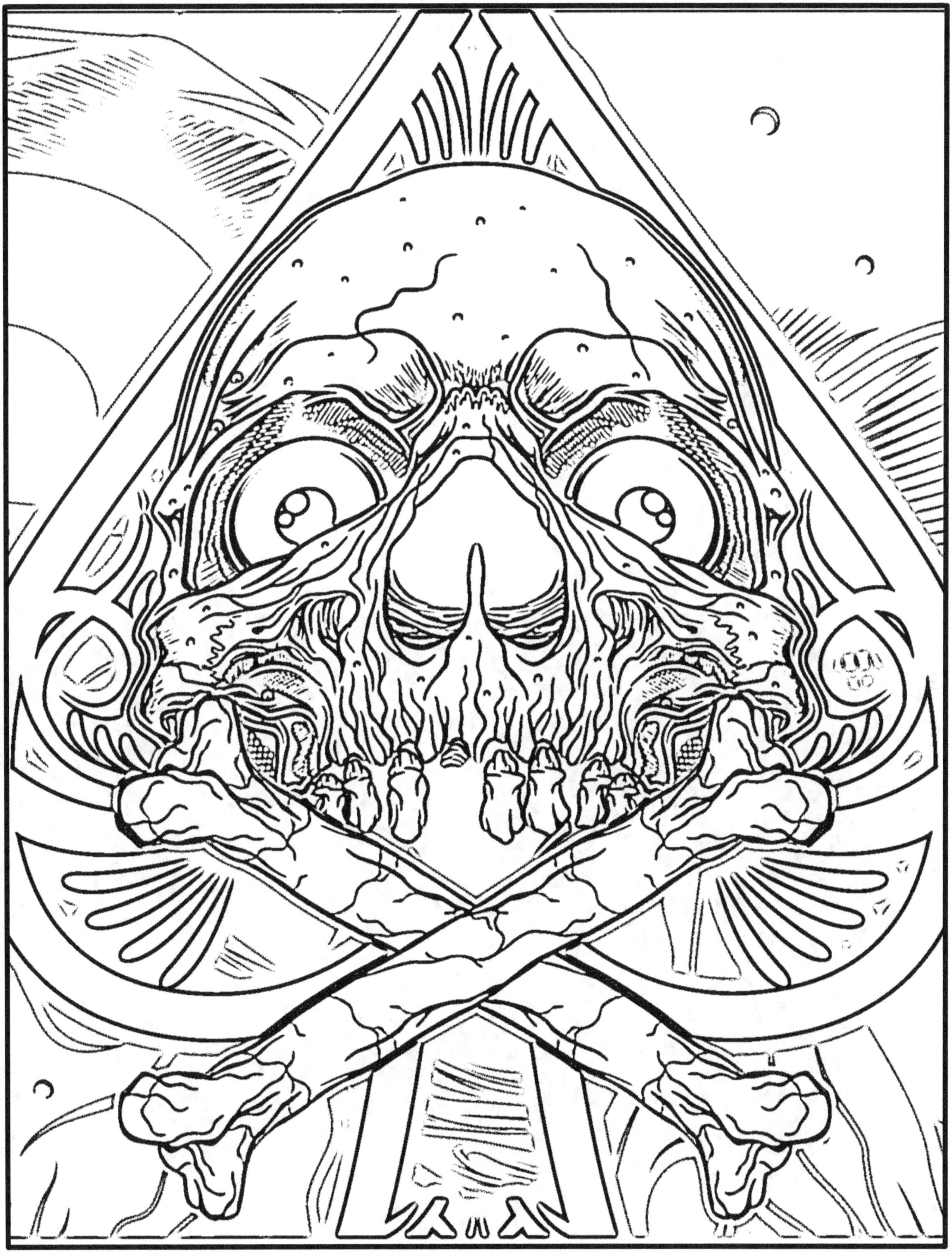

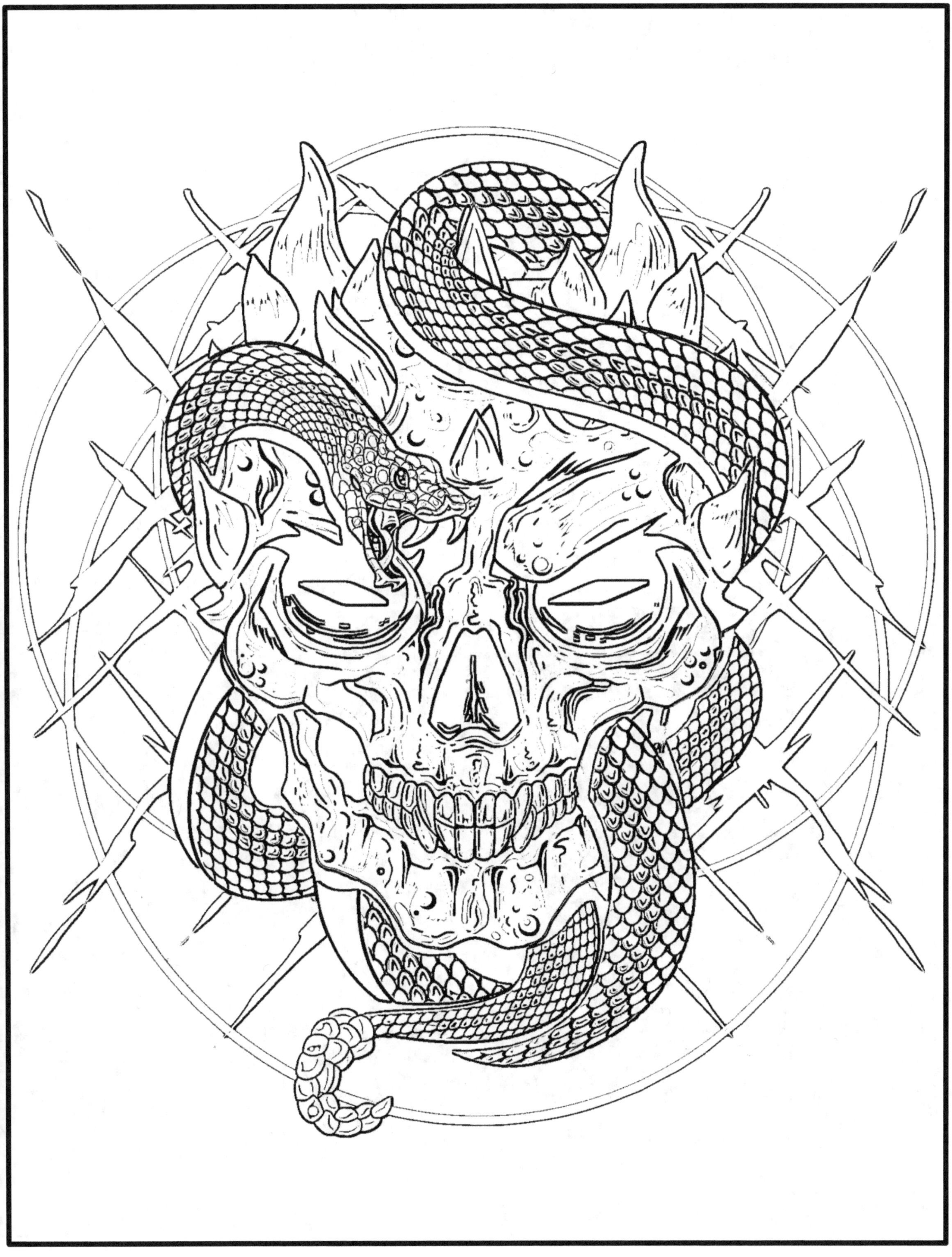

HALLOWEEN

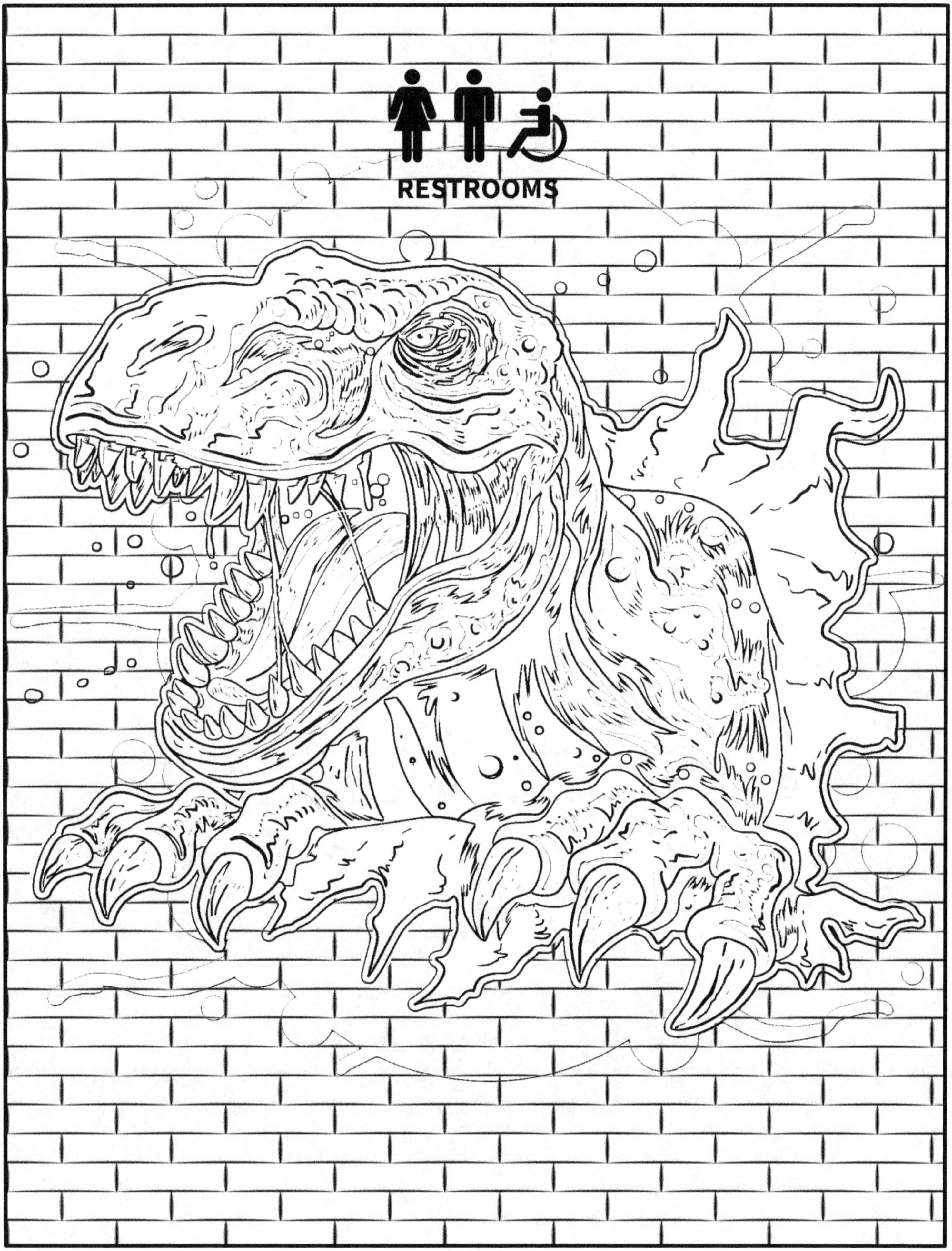
RESTROOMS

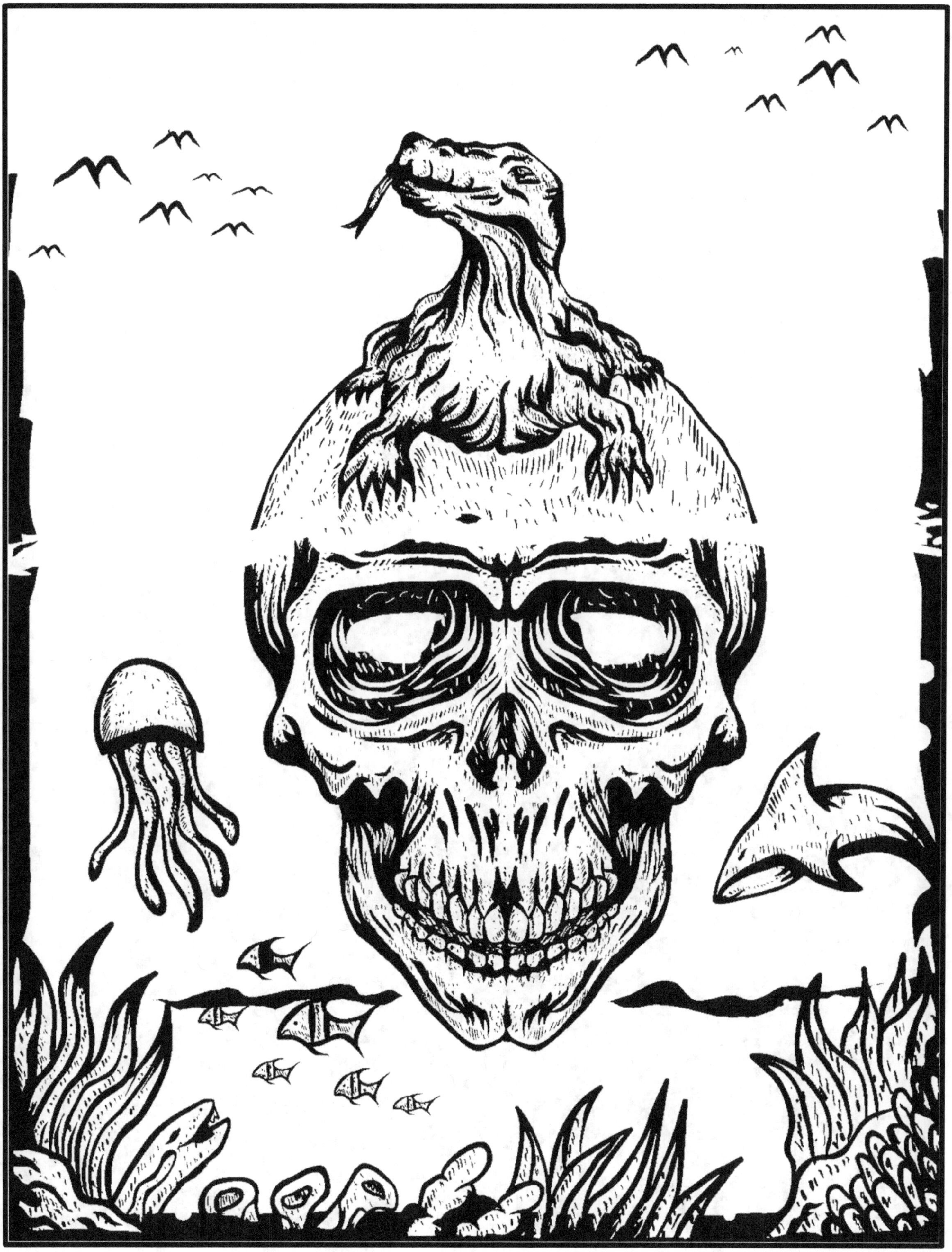

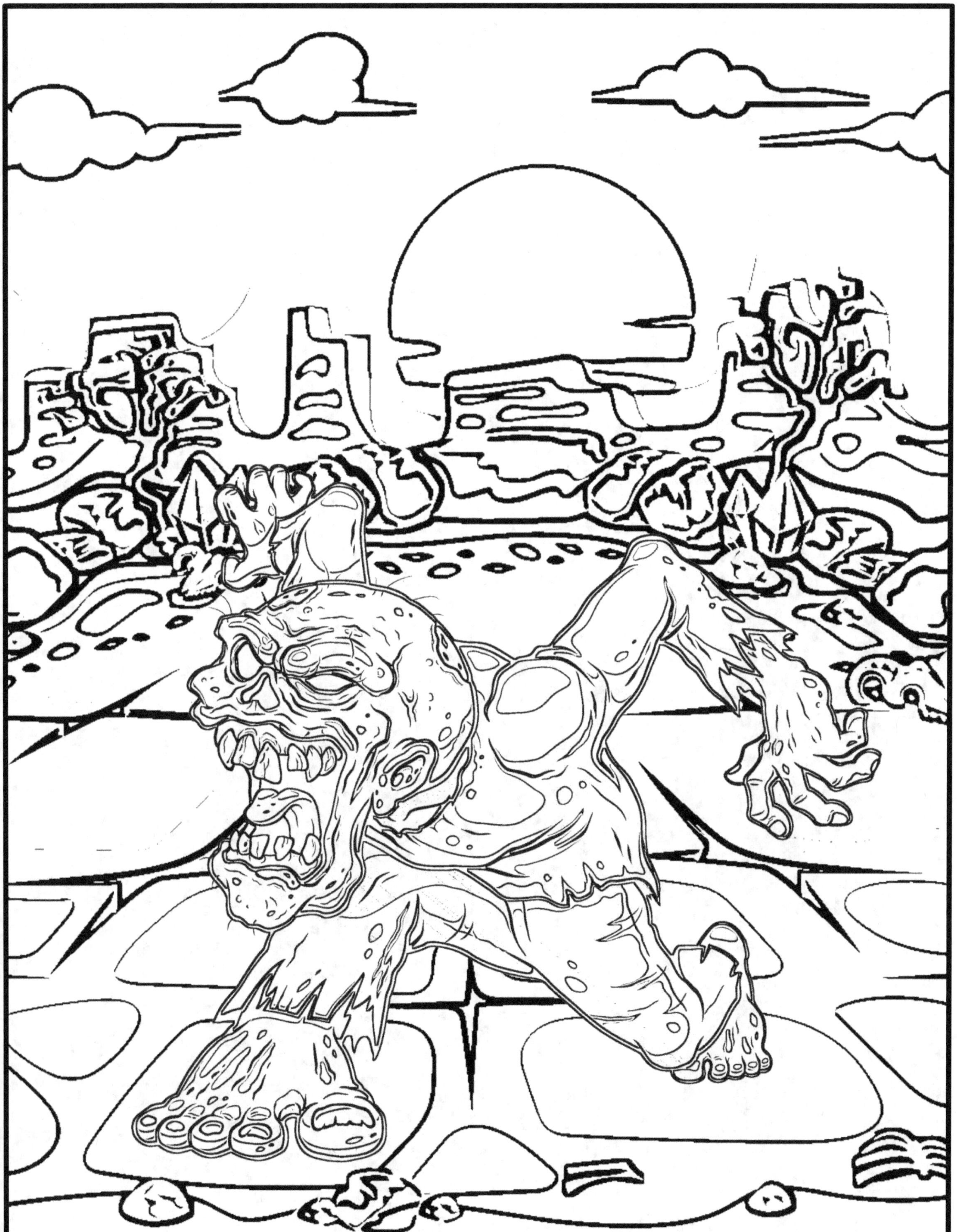

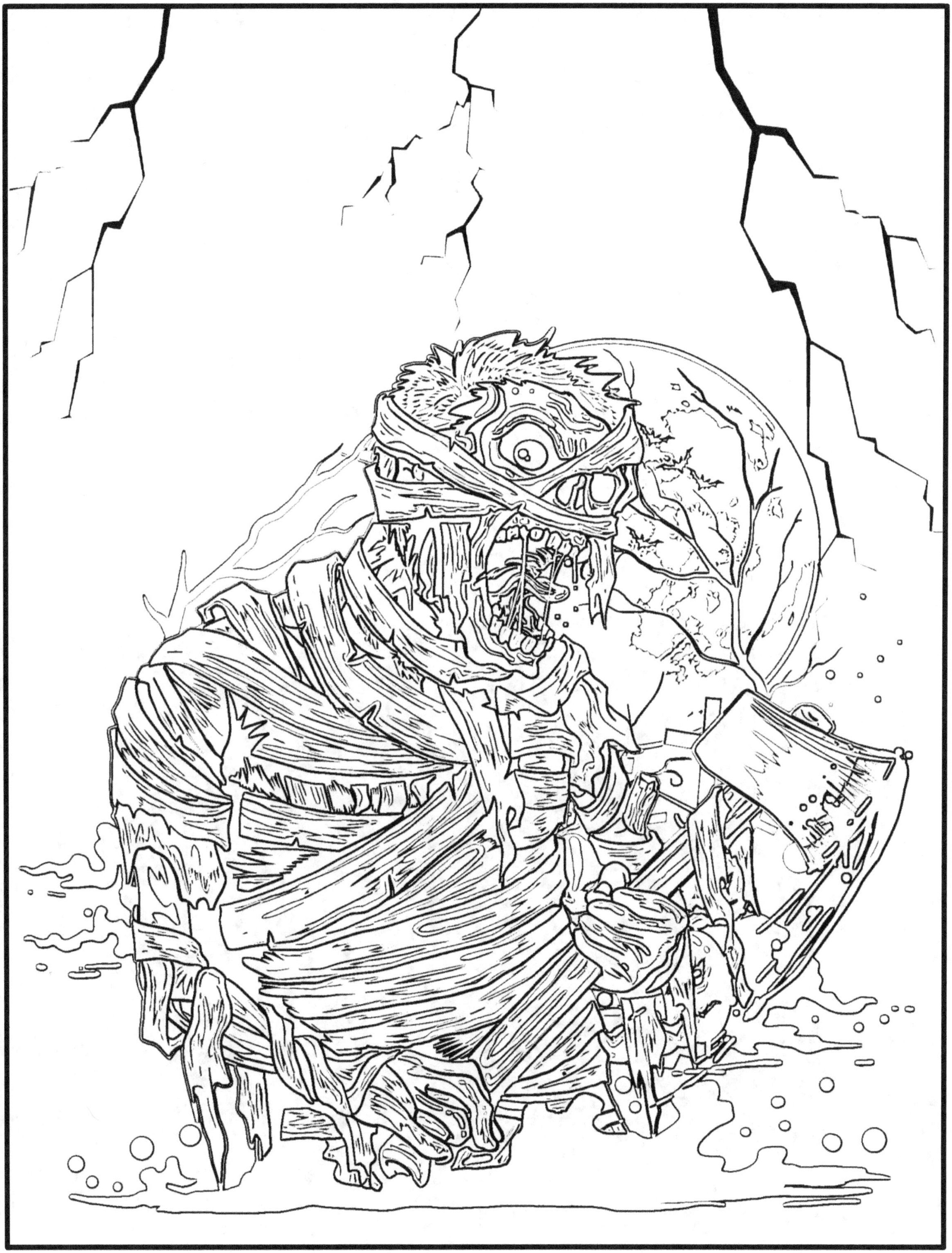

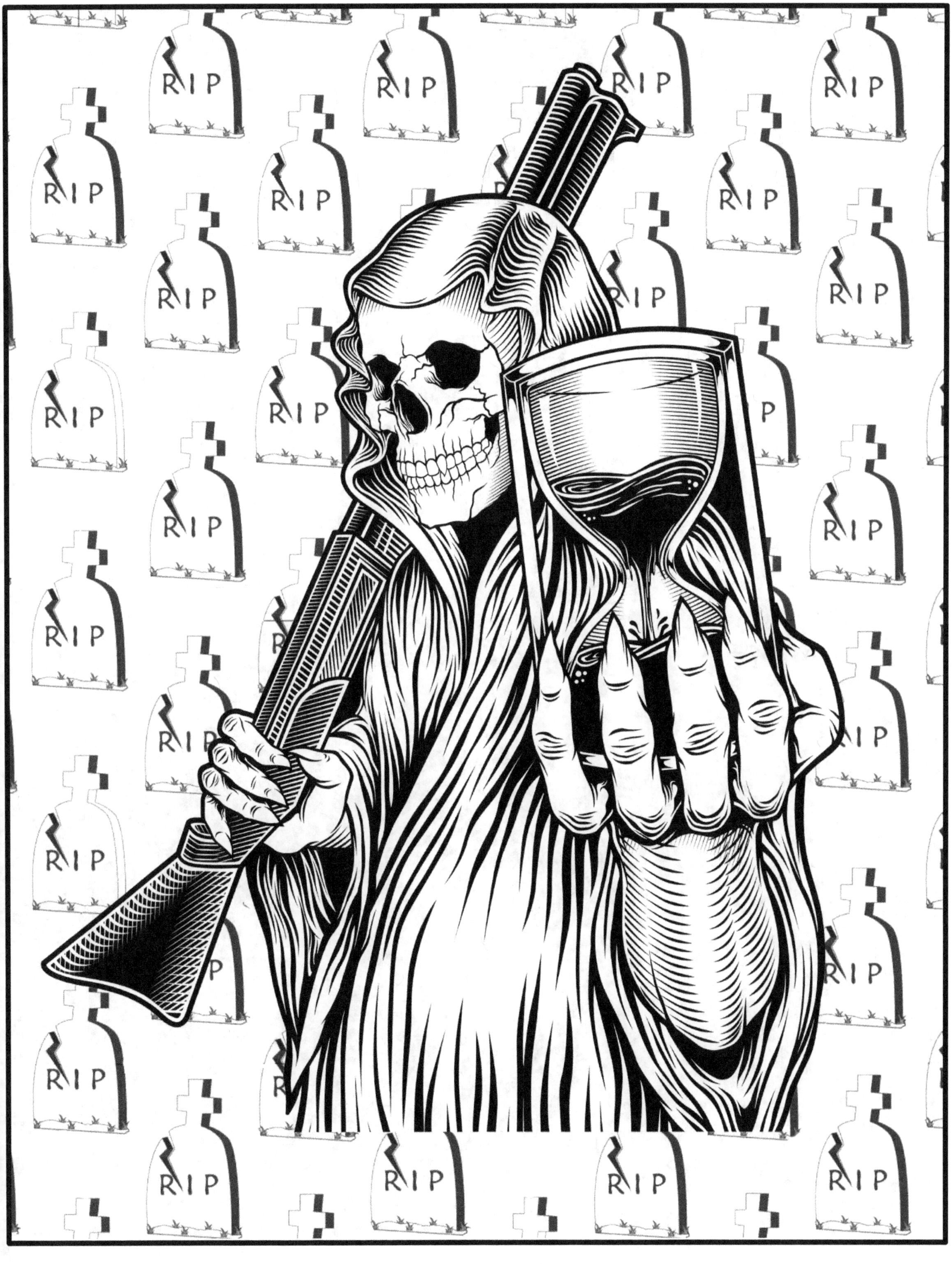
RIP
RIP
RIP
RIP
RIP
RIP
RIP
RIP
RIP
RIP
RIP
RIP
RIP
RIP
RIP
RIP
RIP
RIP
RIP
RIP

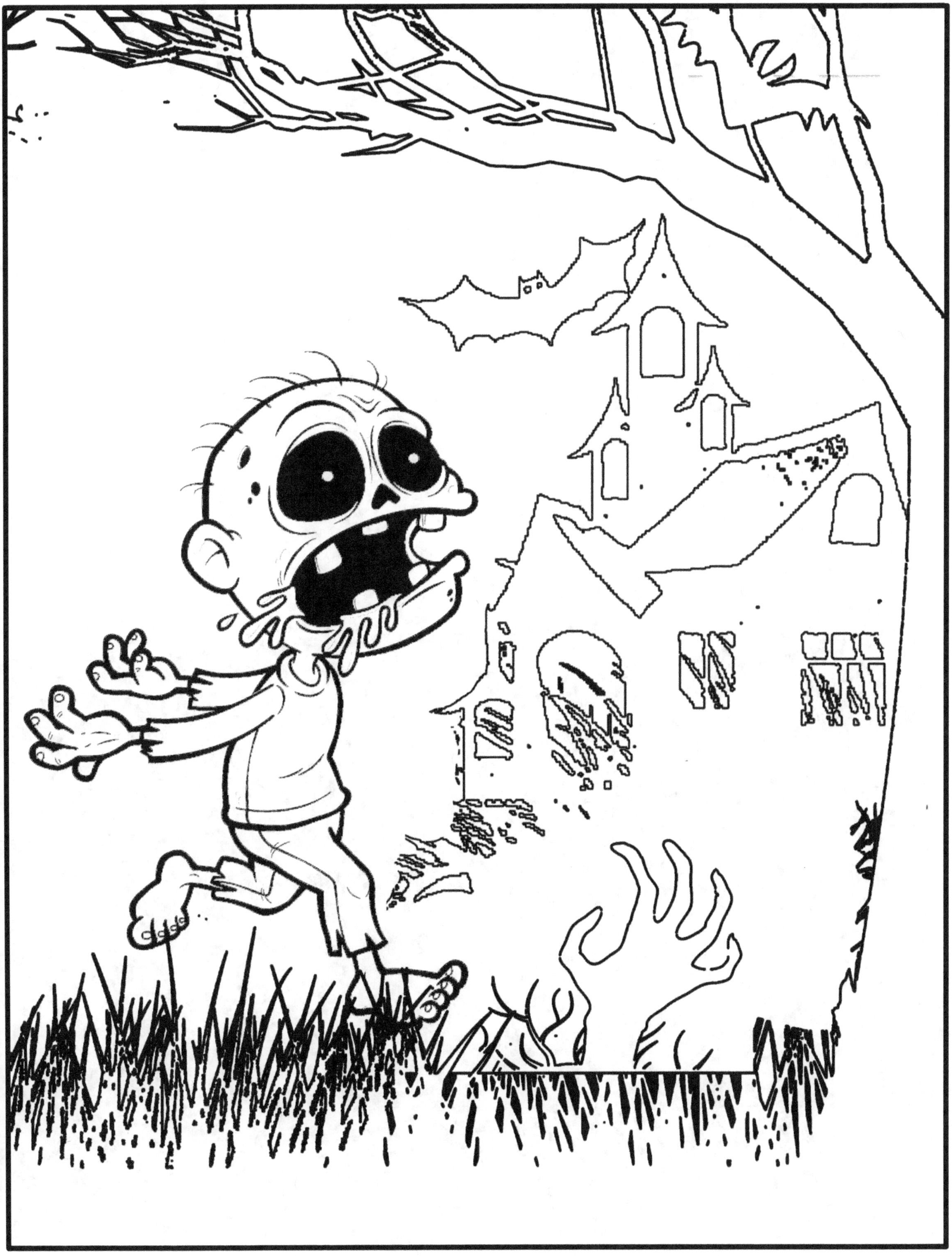

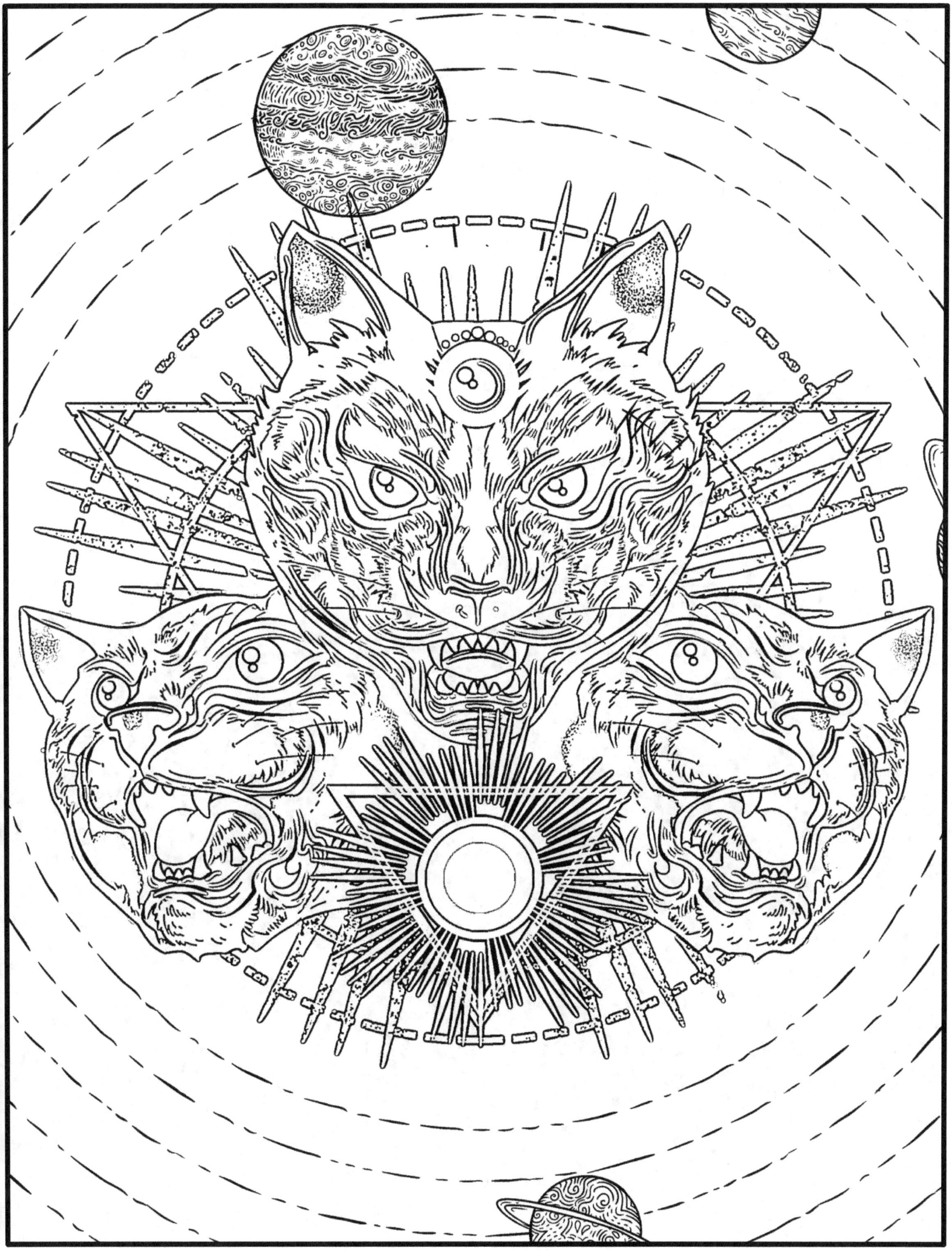

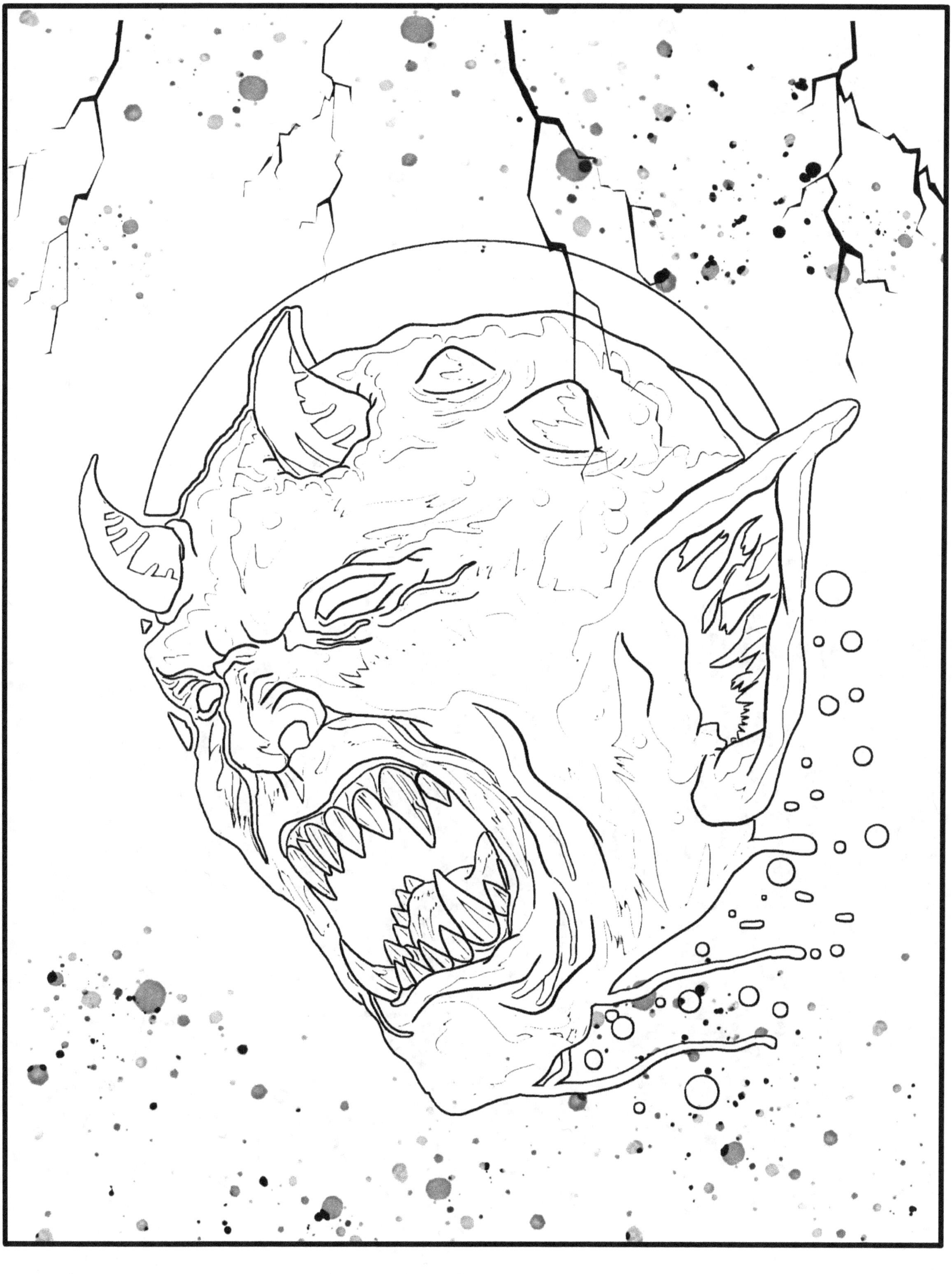

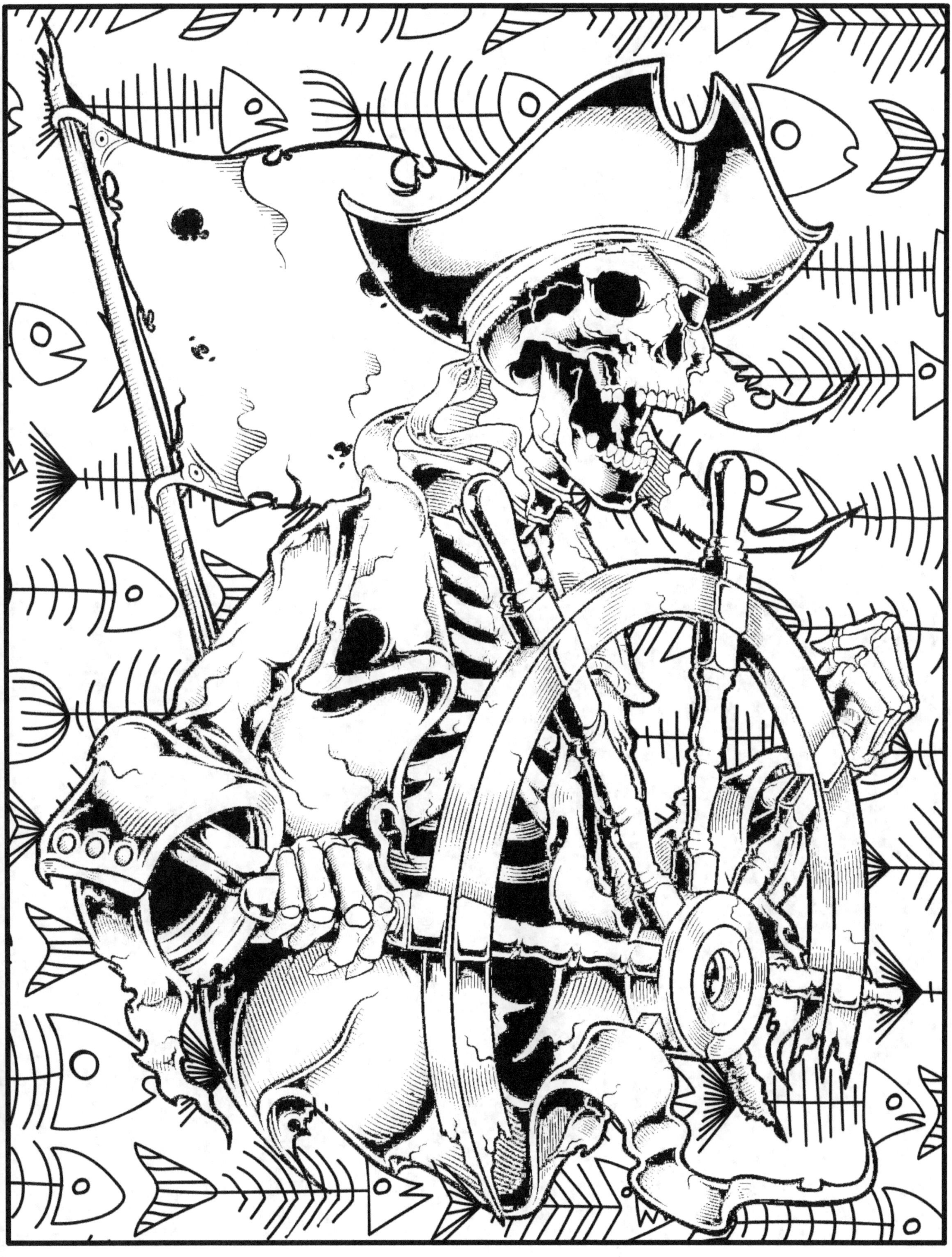

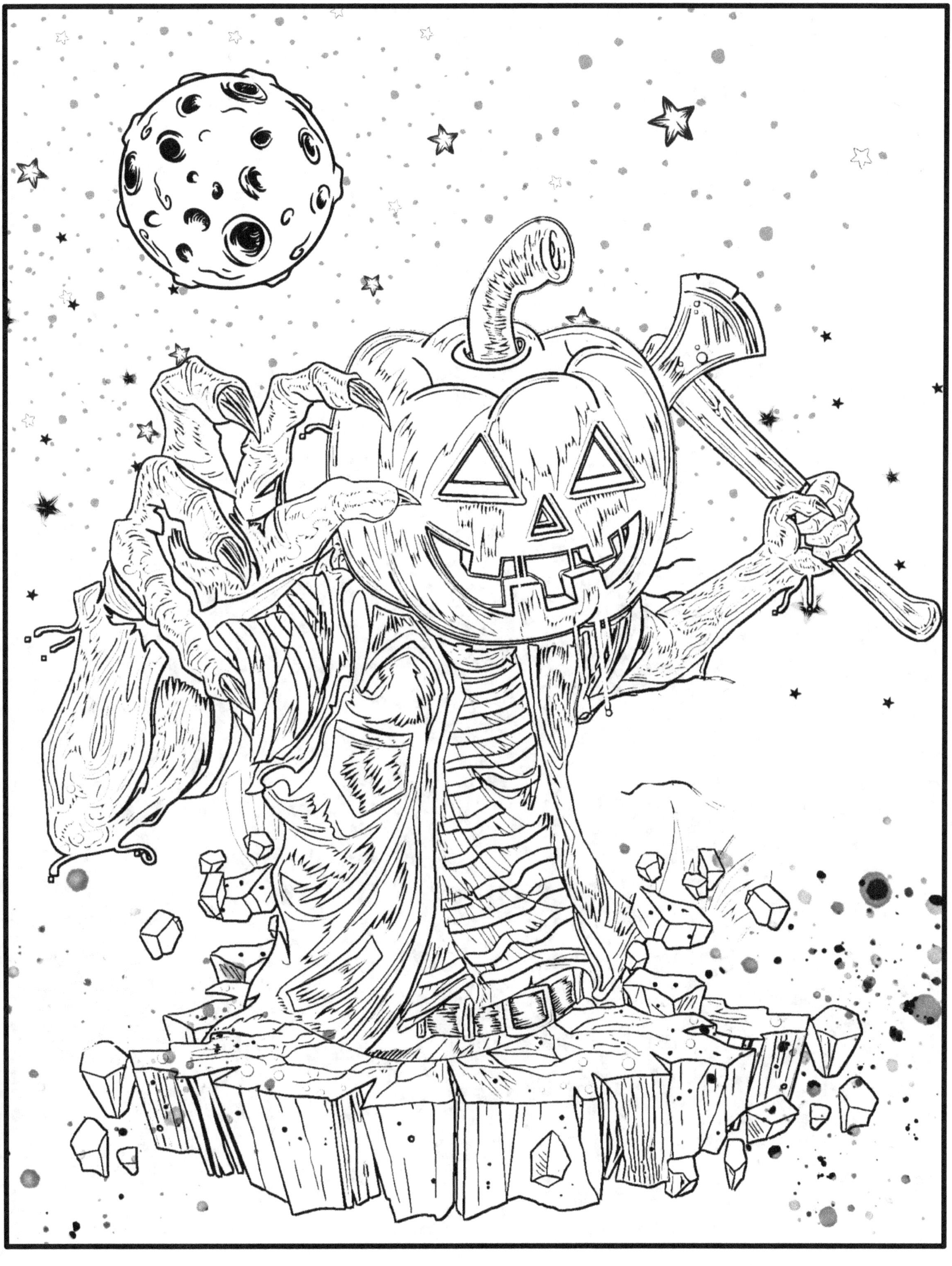

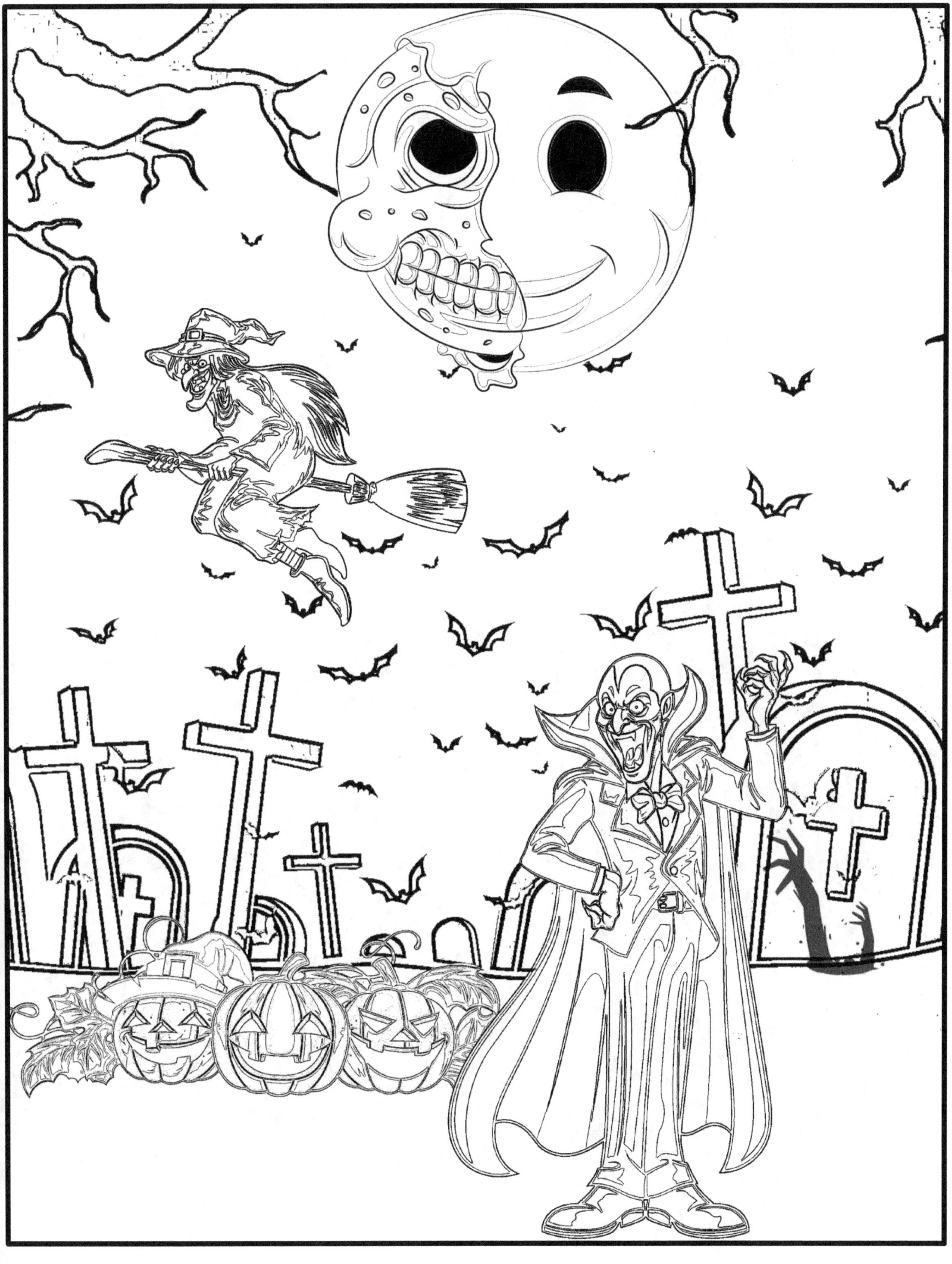

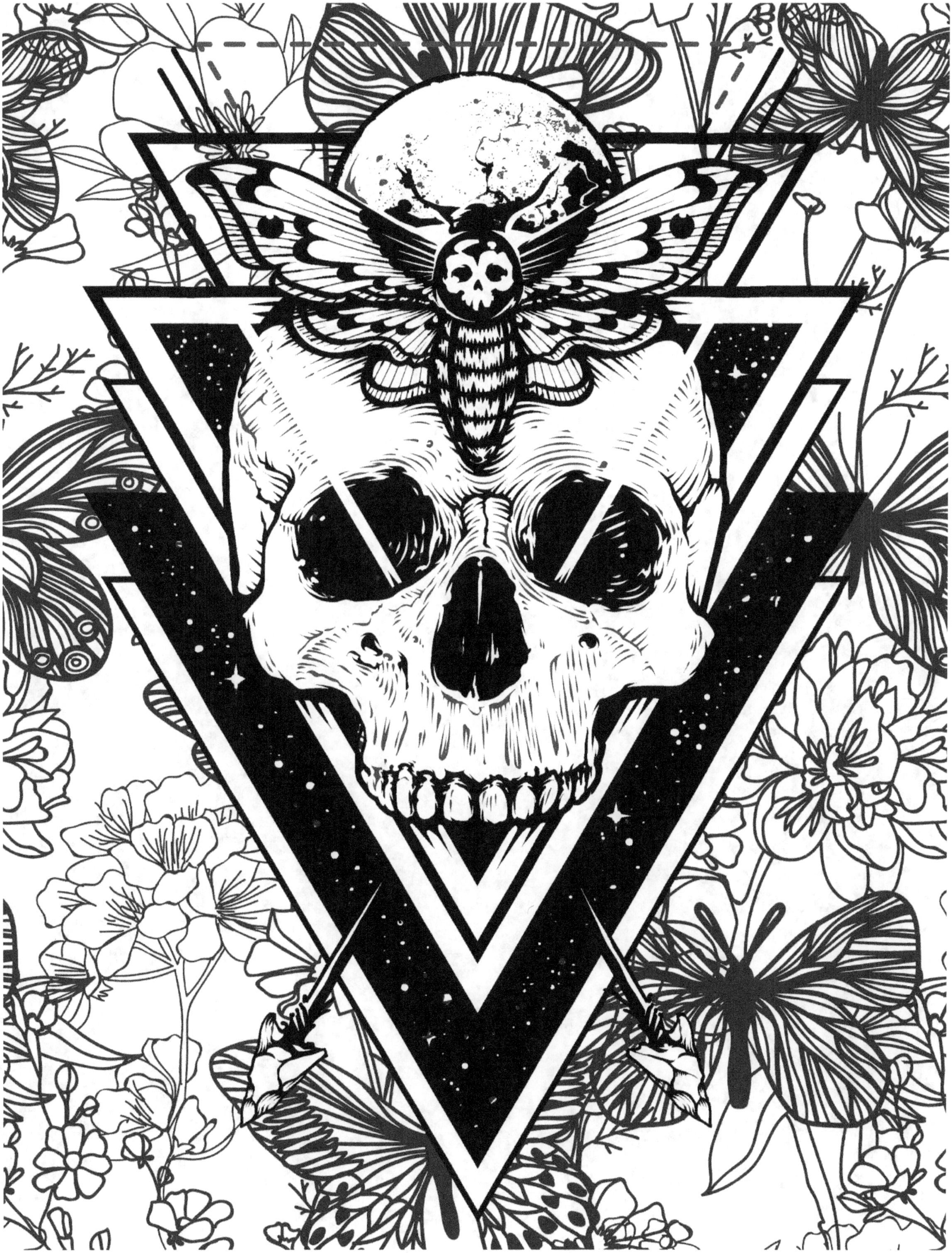

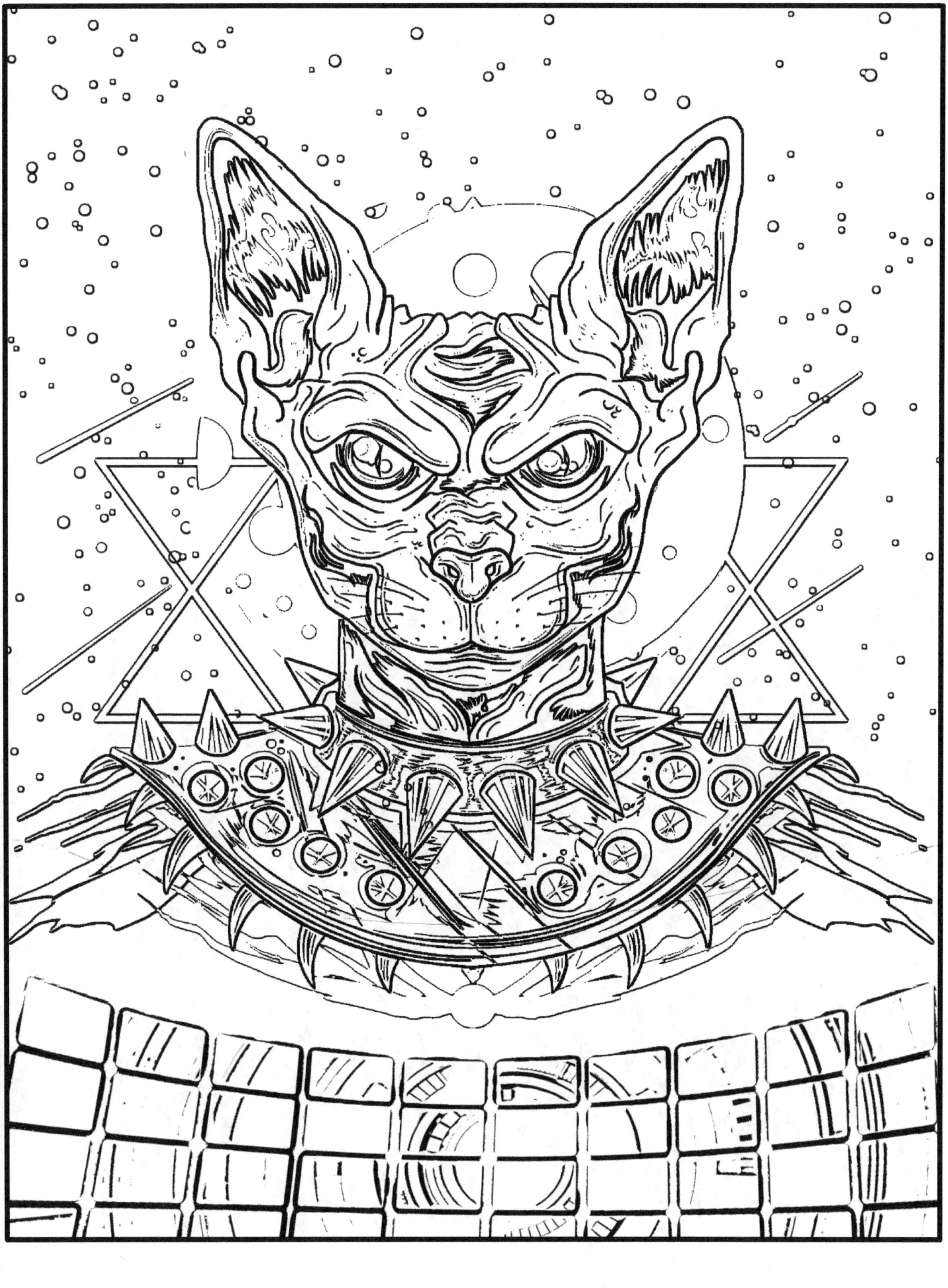

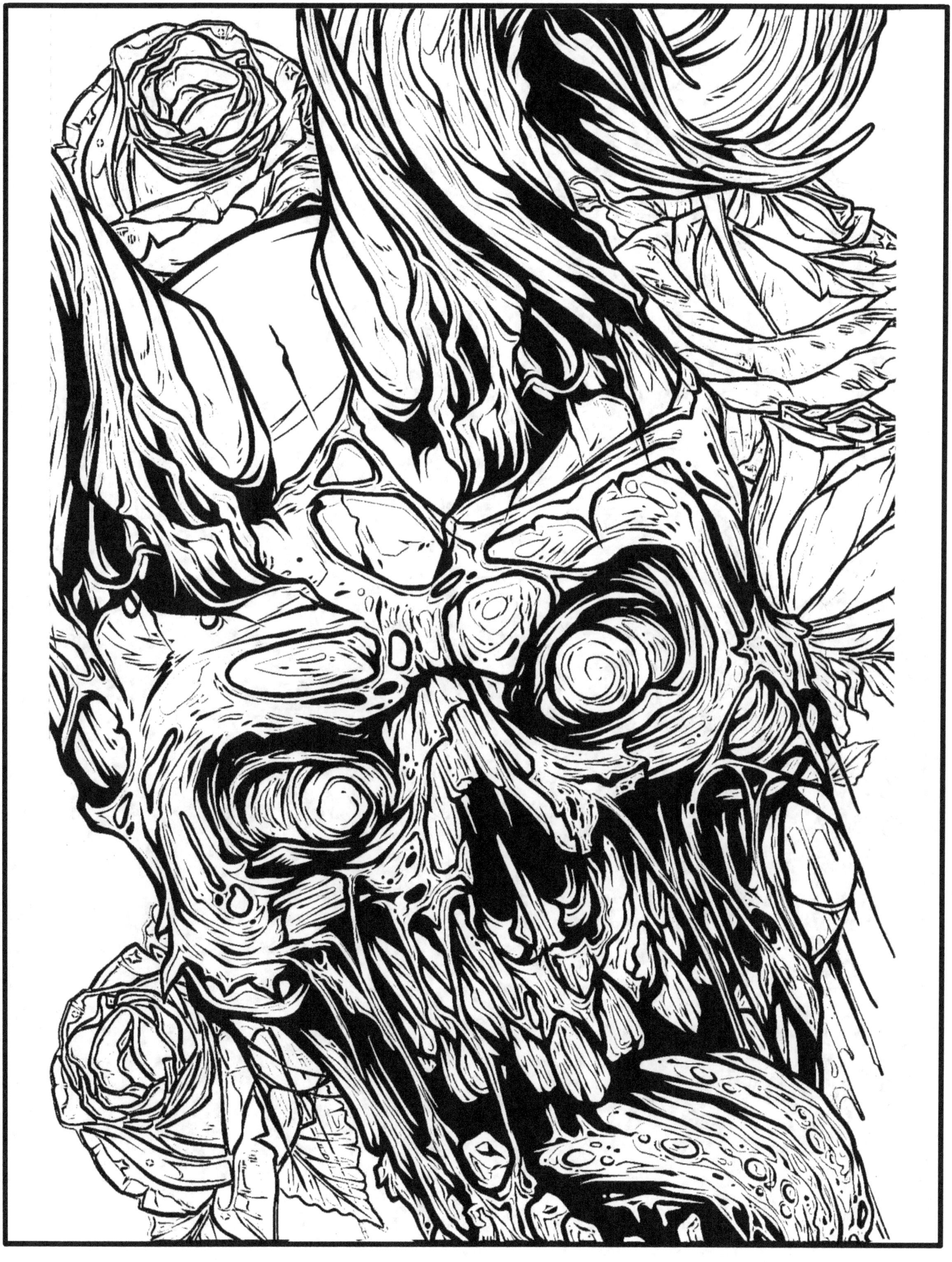

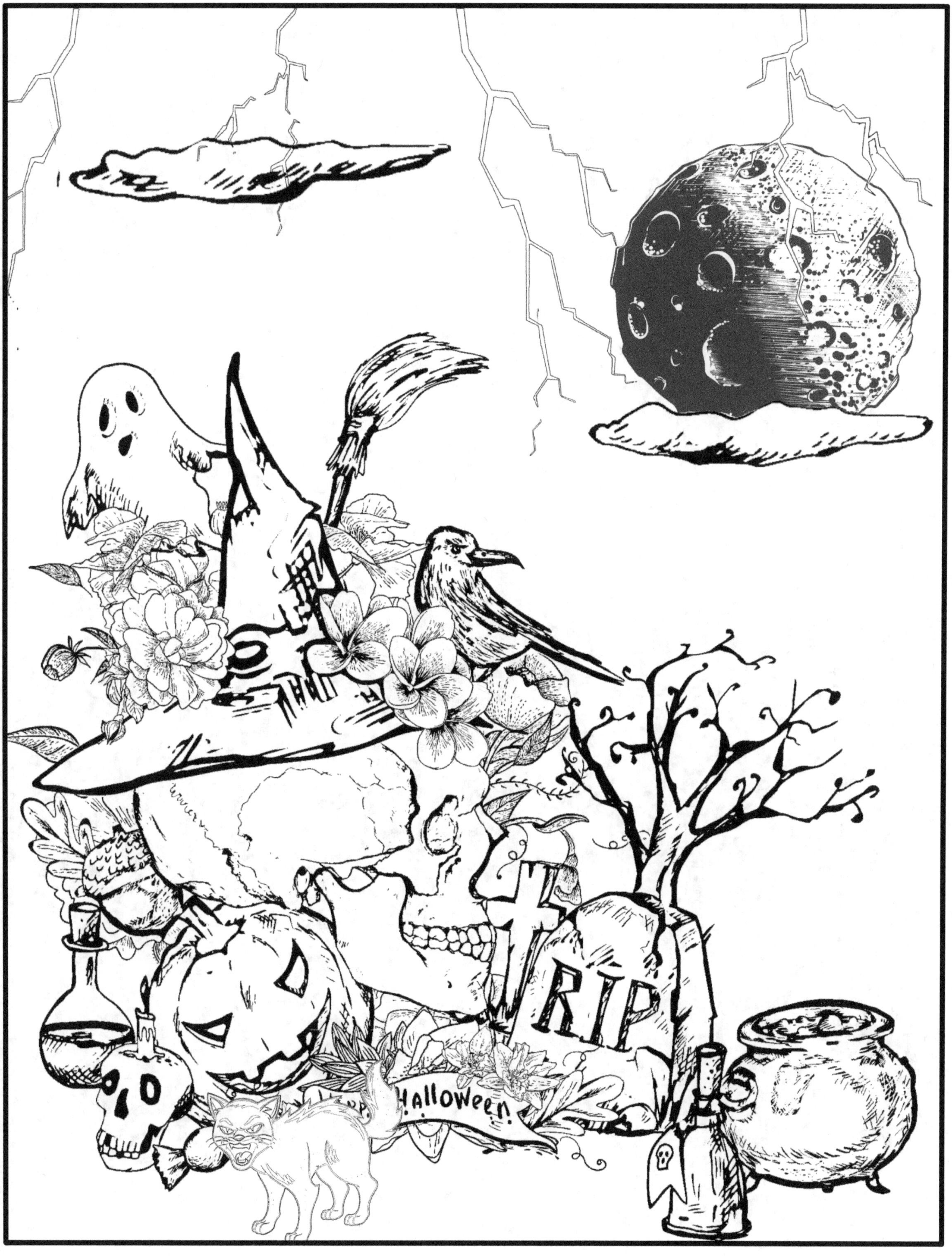
RIP
Halloween!

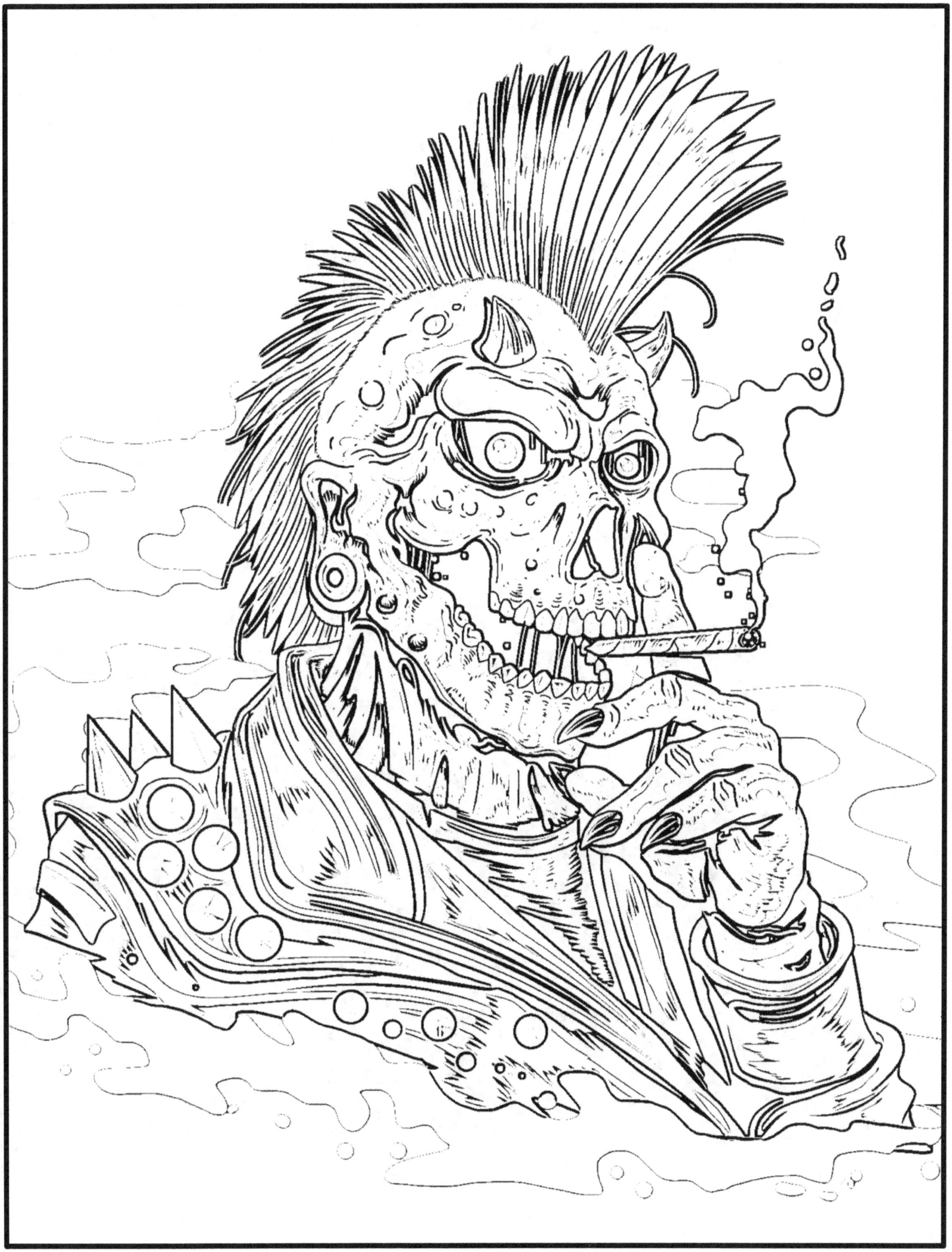

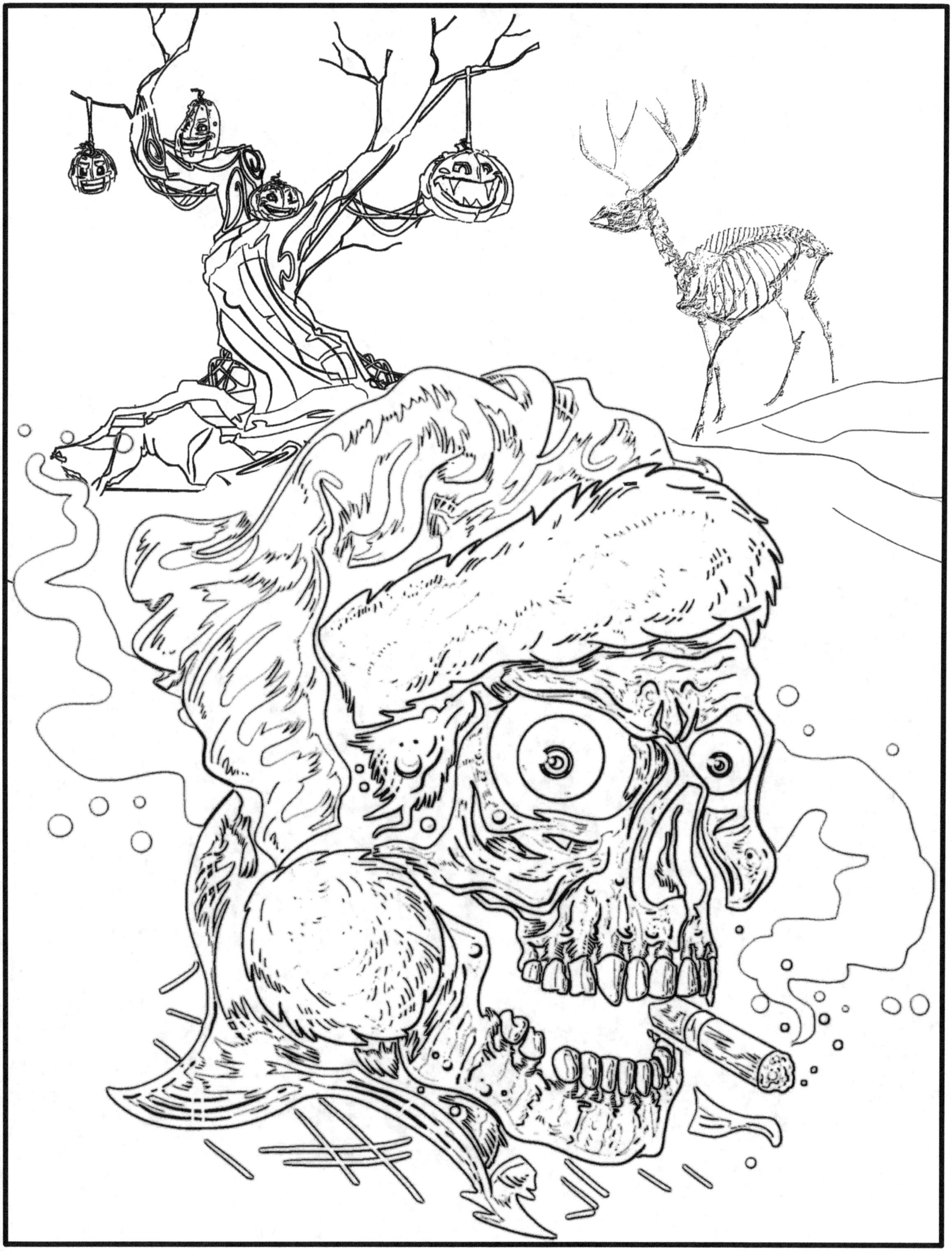

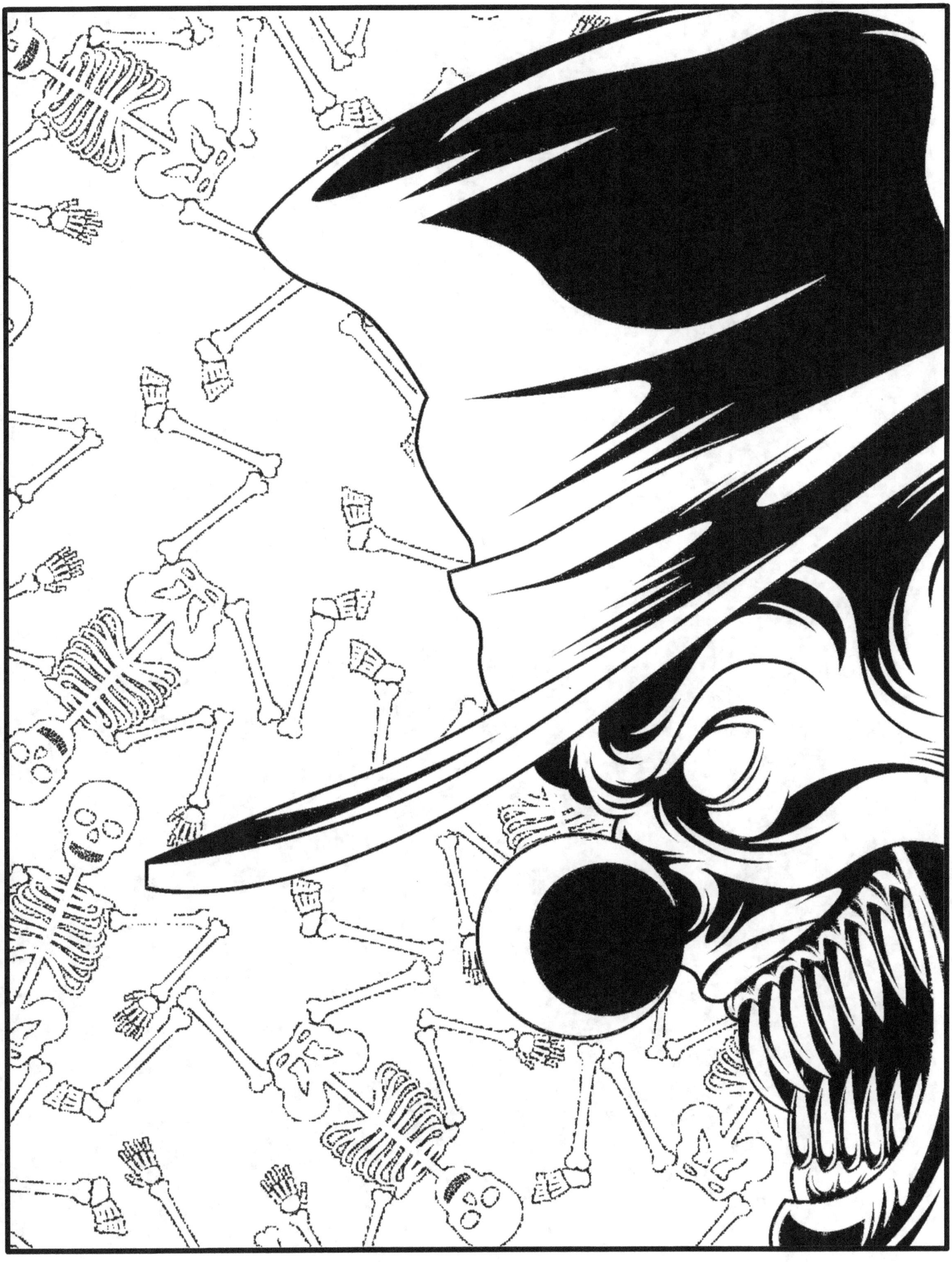

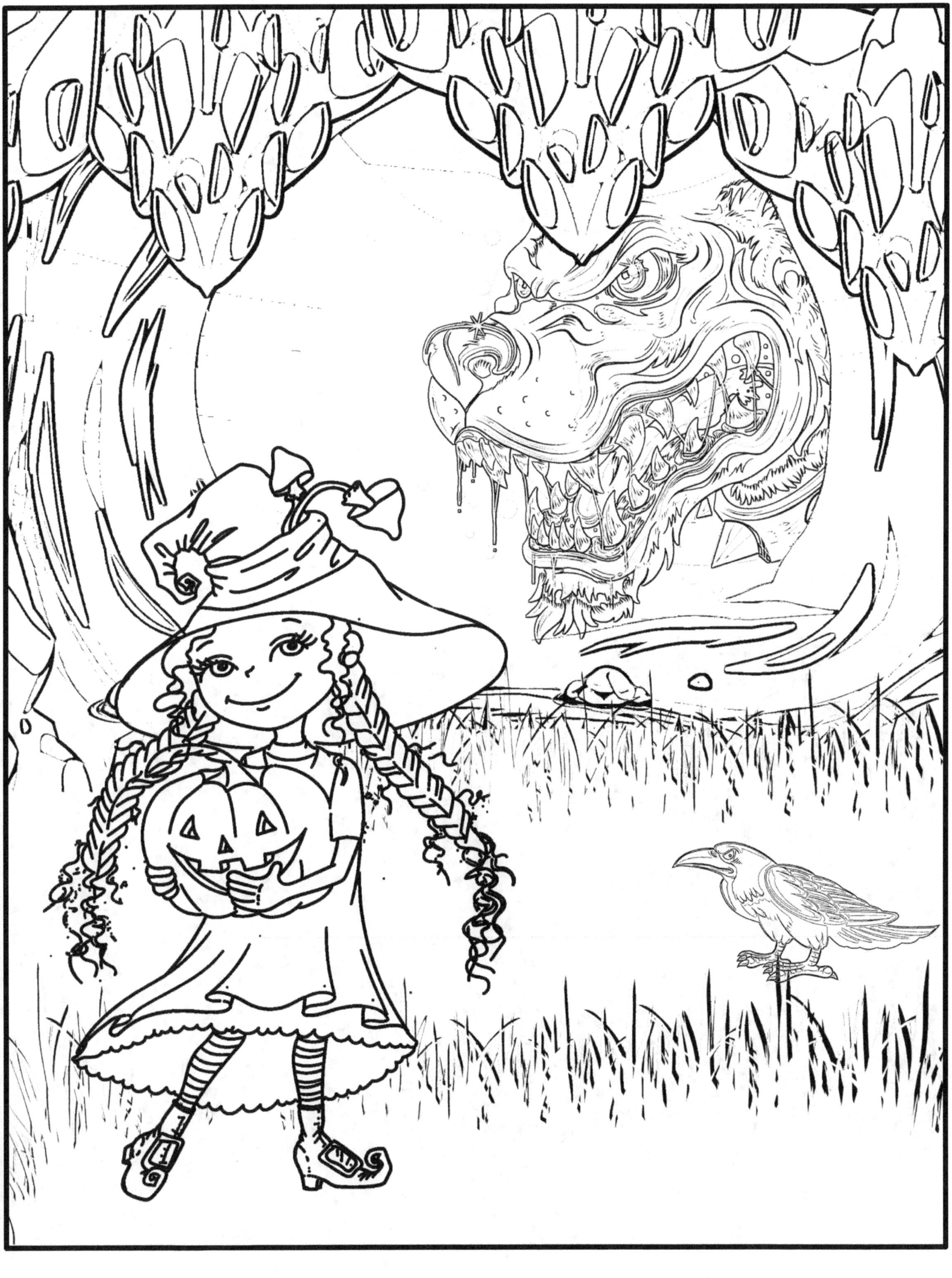

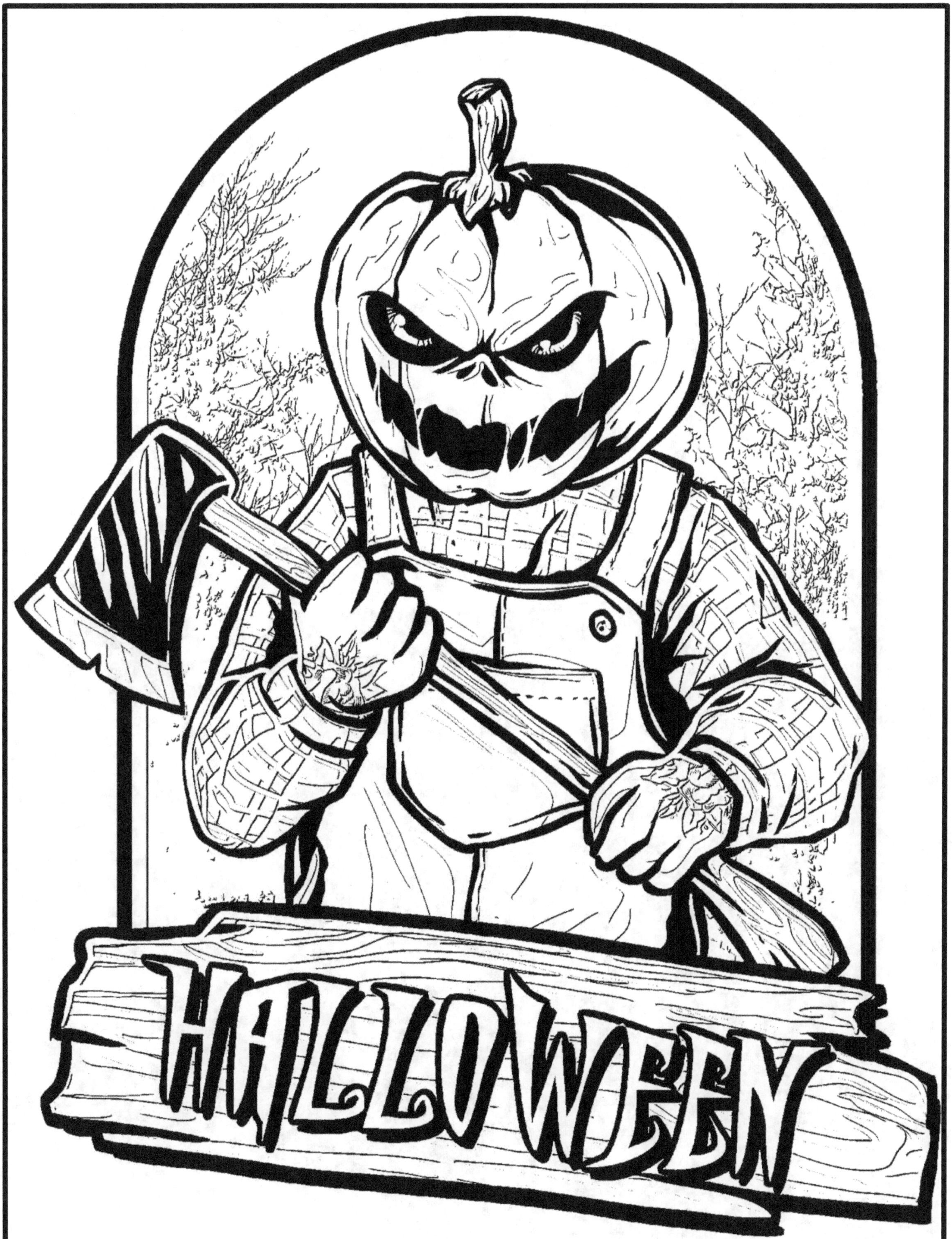
HALLOWEEN

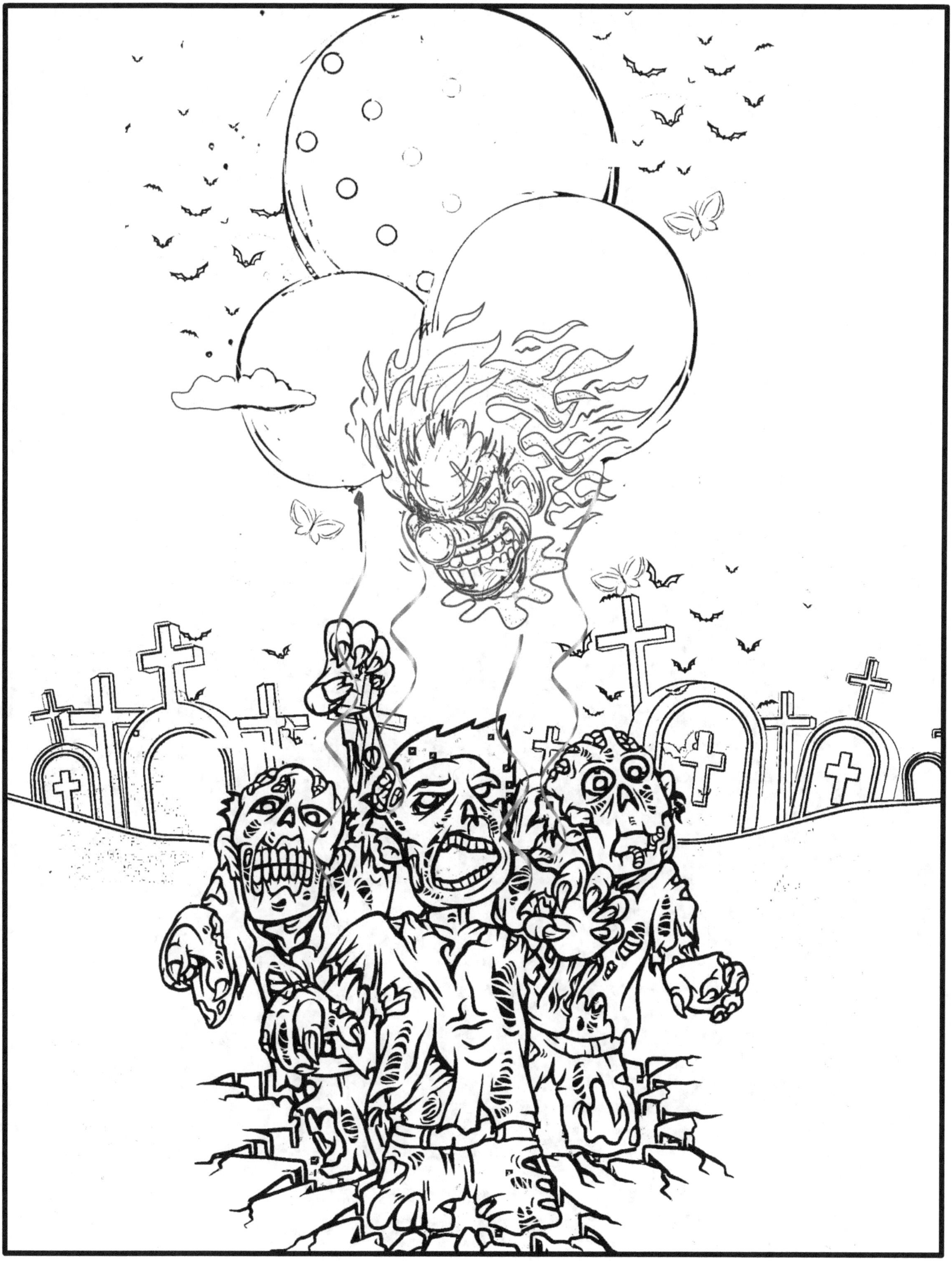

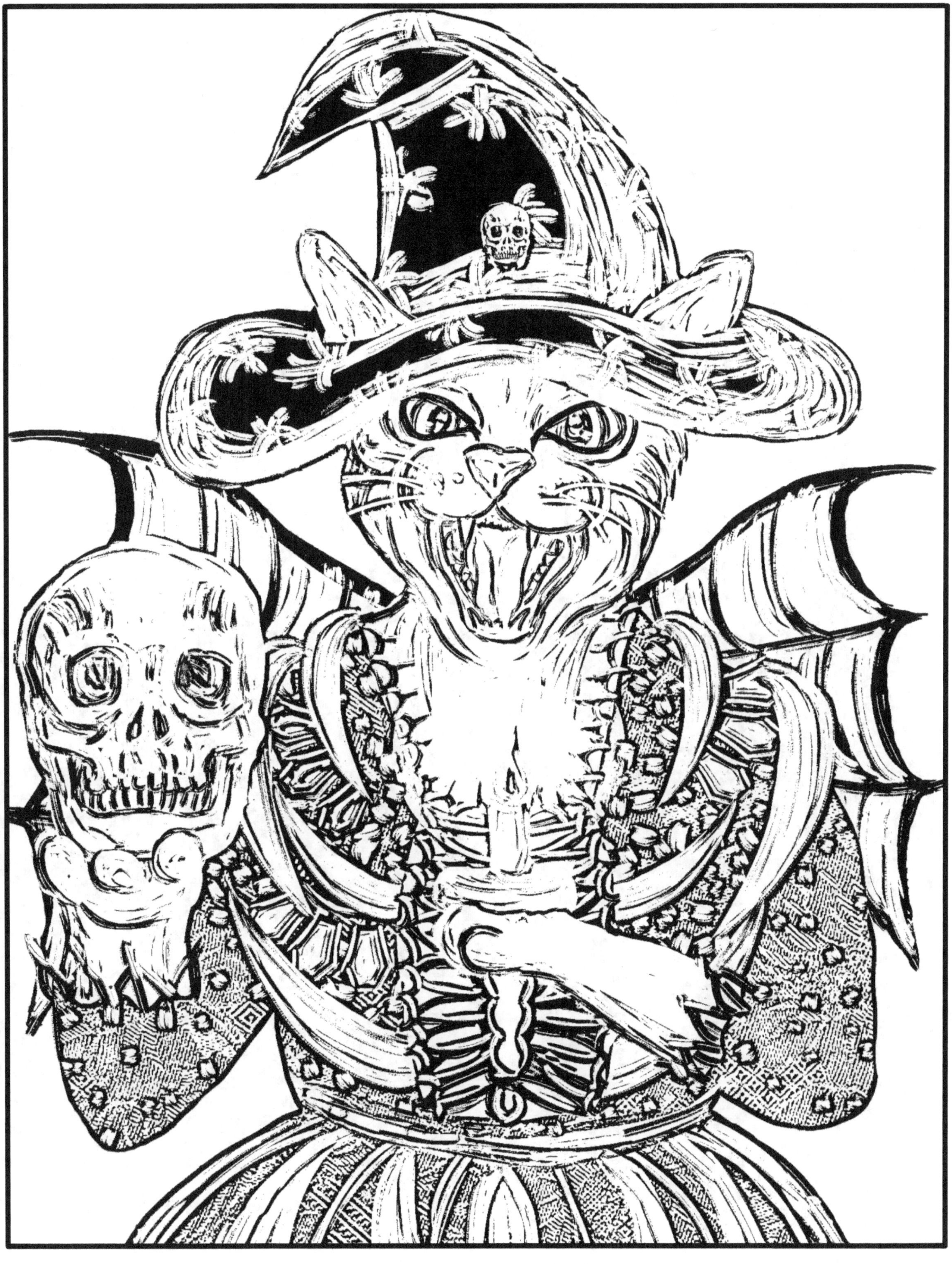

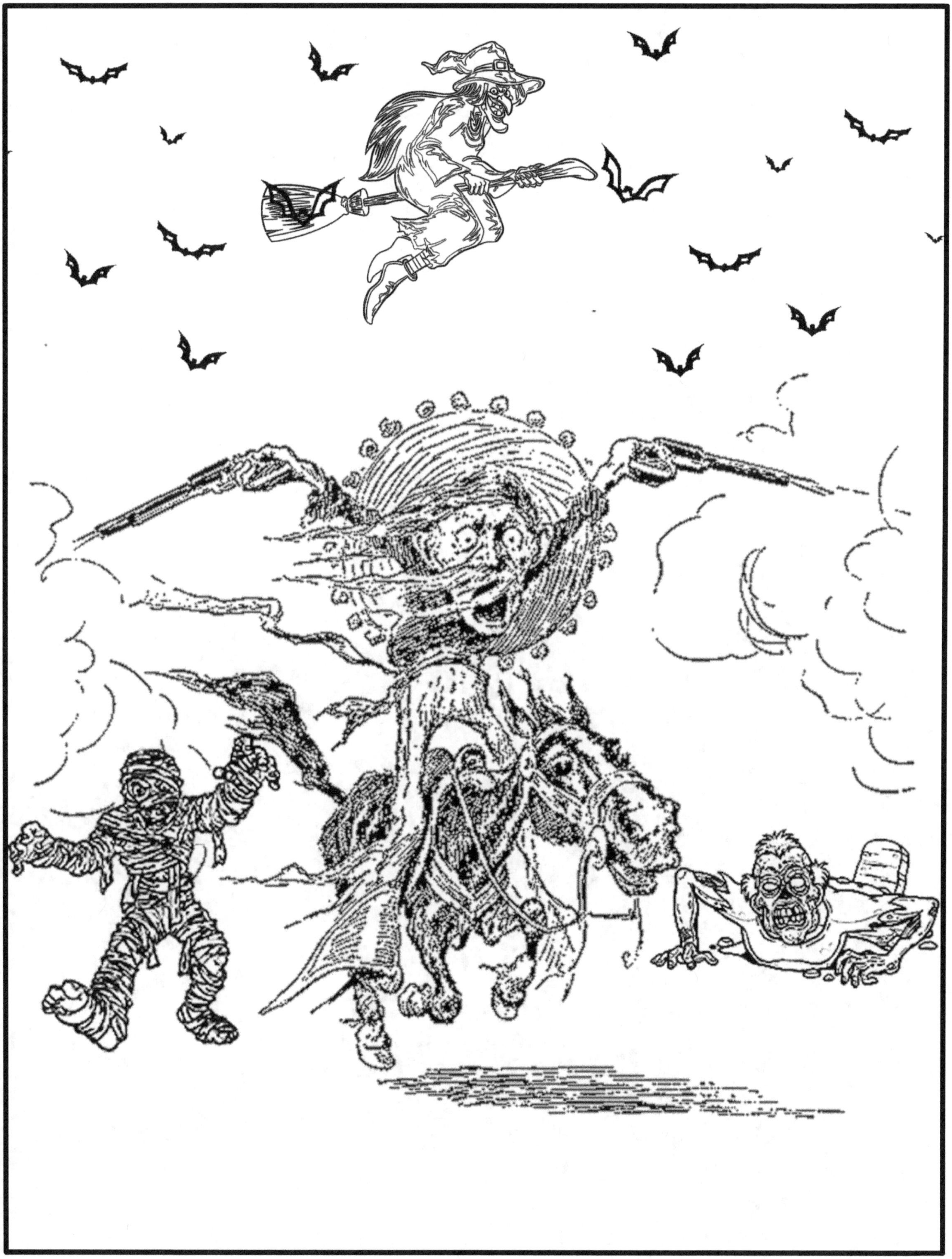

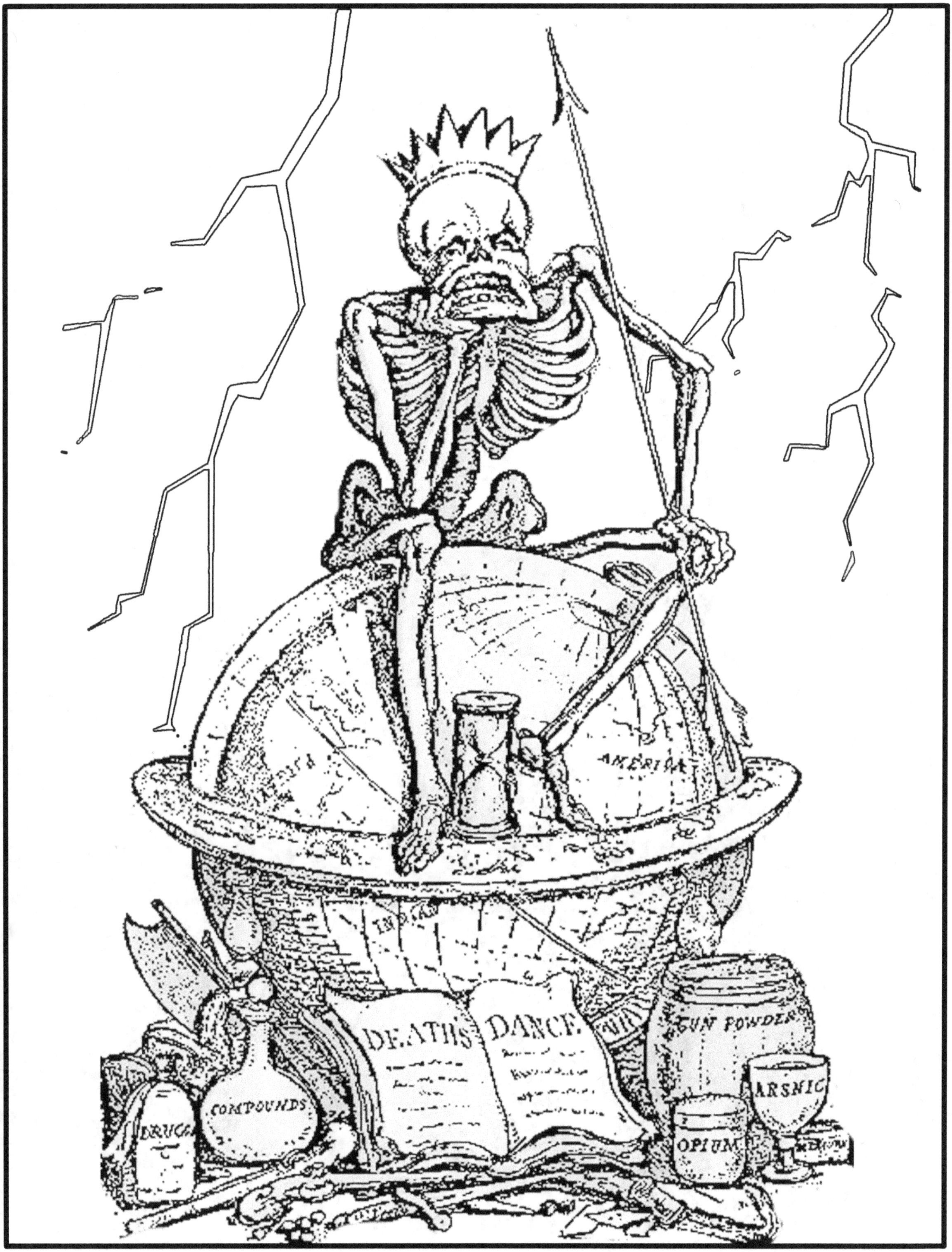
DEATHS
DANCE
AMERICA
INDIA
GUN POWDER
ARSNIC
COMPOUNDS
OPIUM

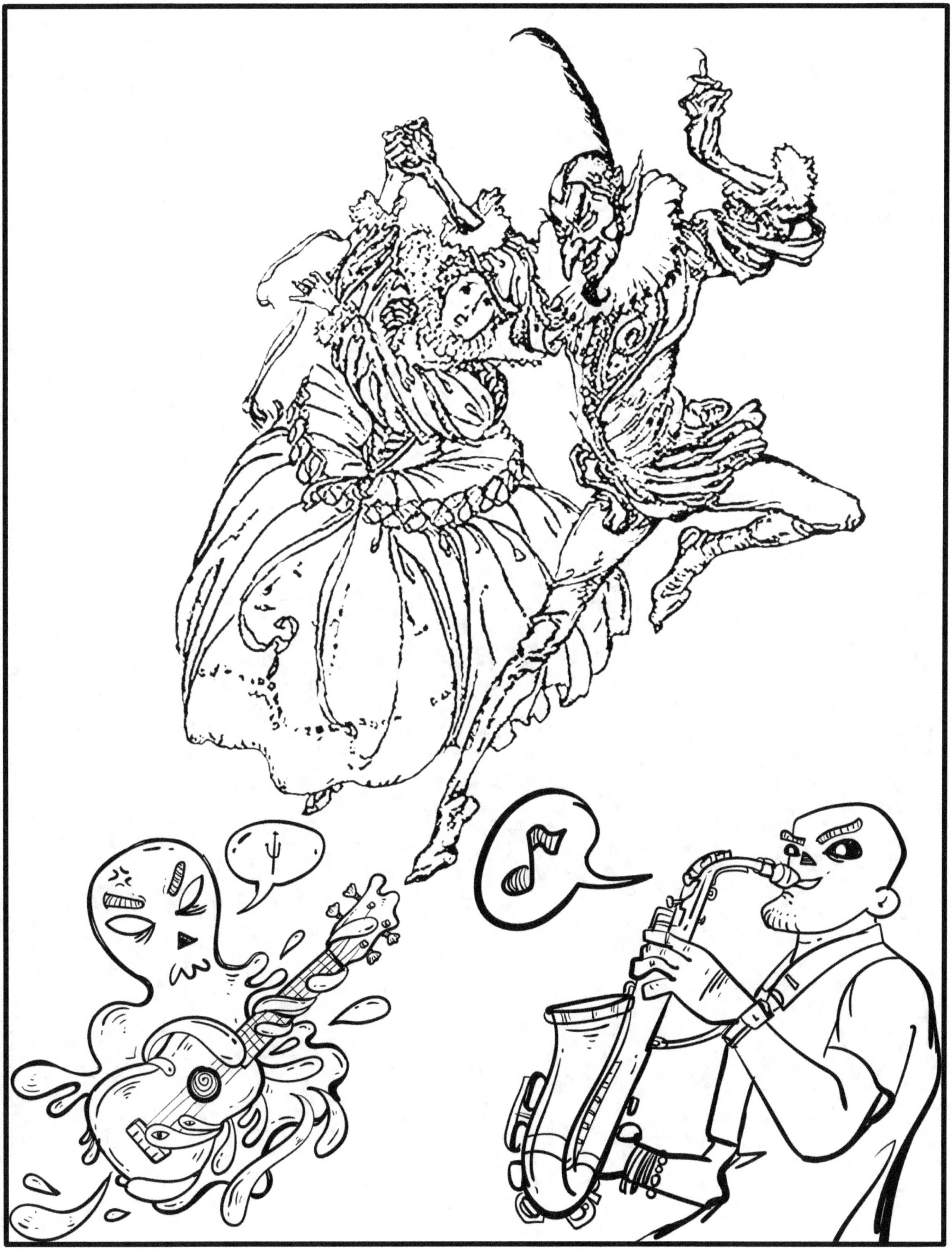

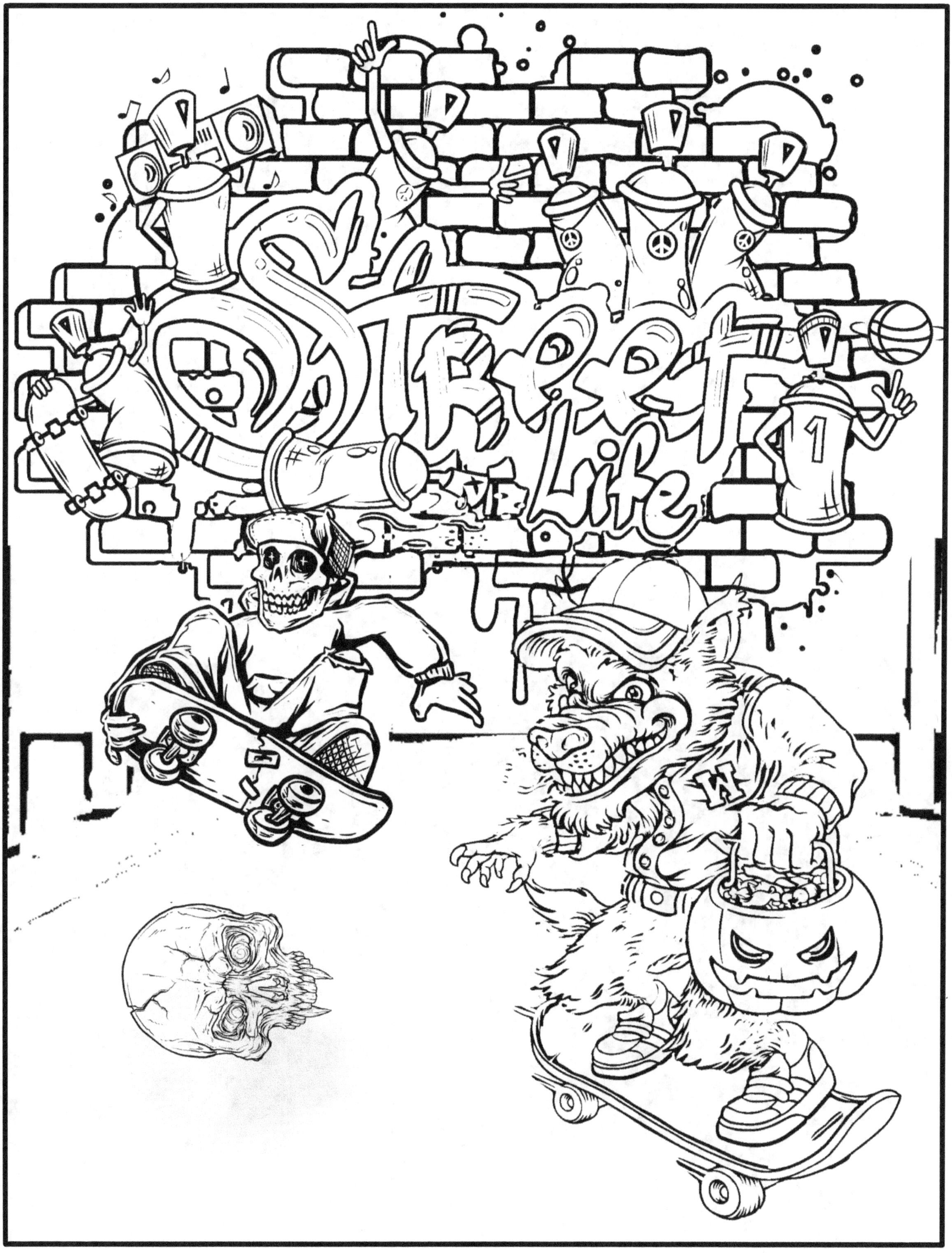
Street
Life

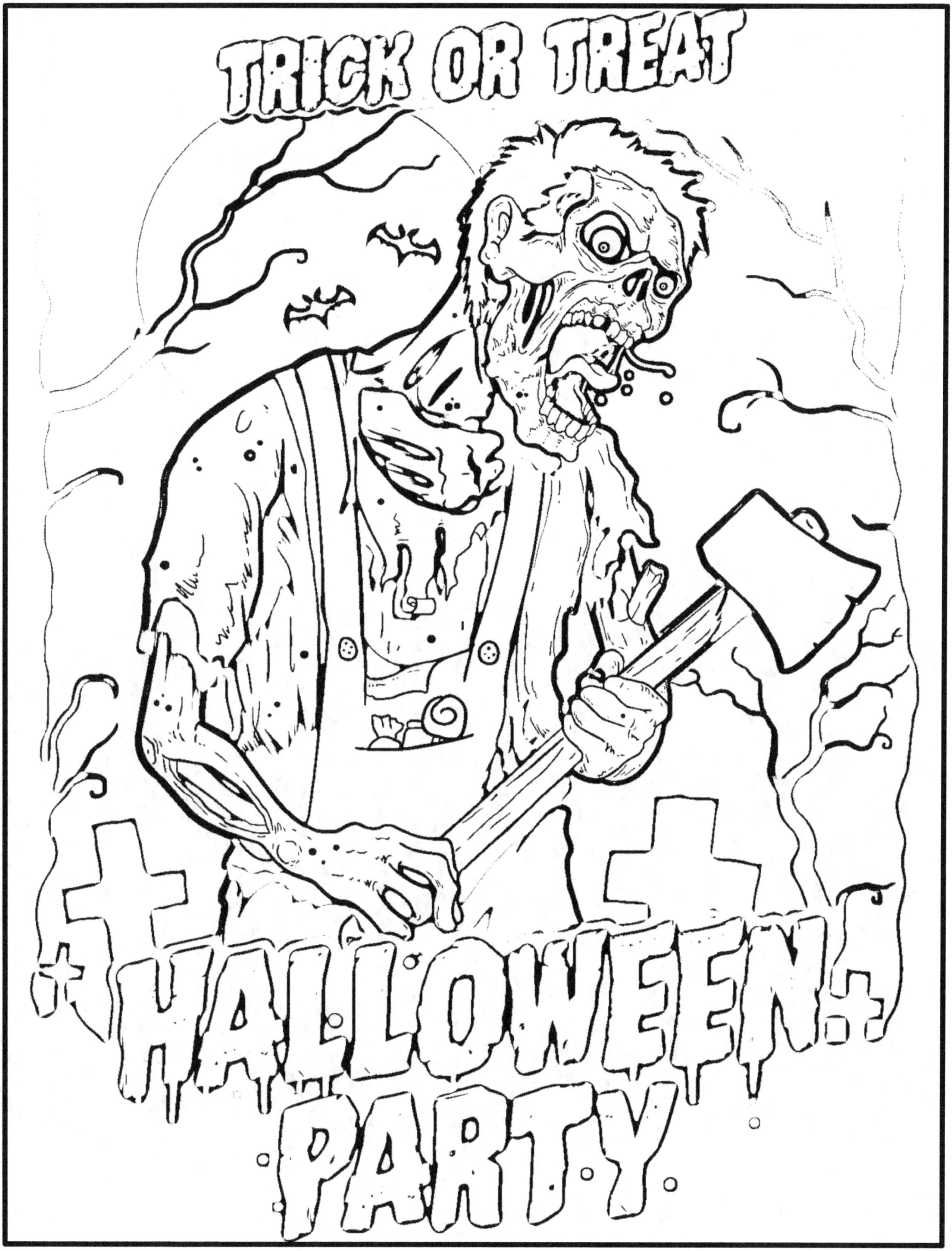
TRICK OR TREAT
HALLOWEEN
PARTY

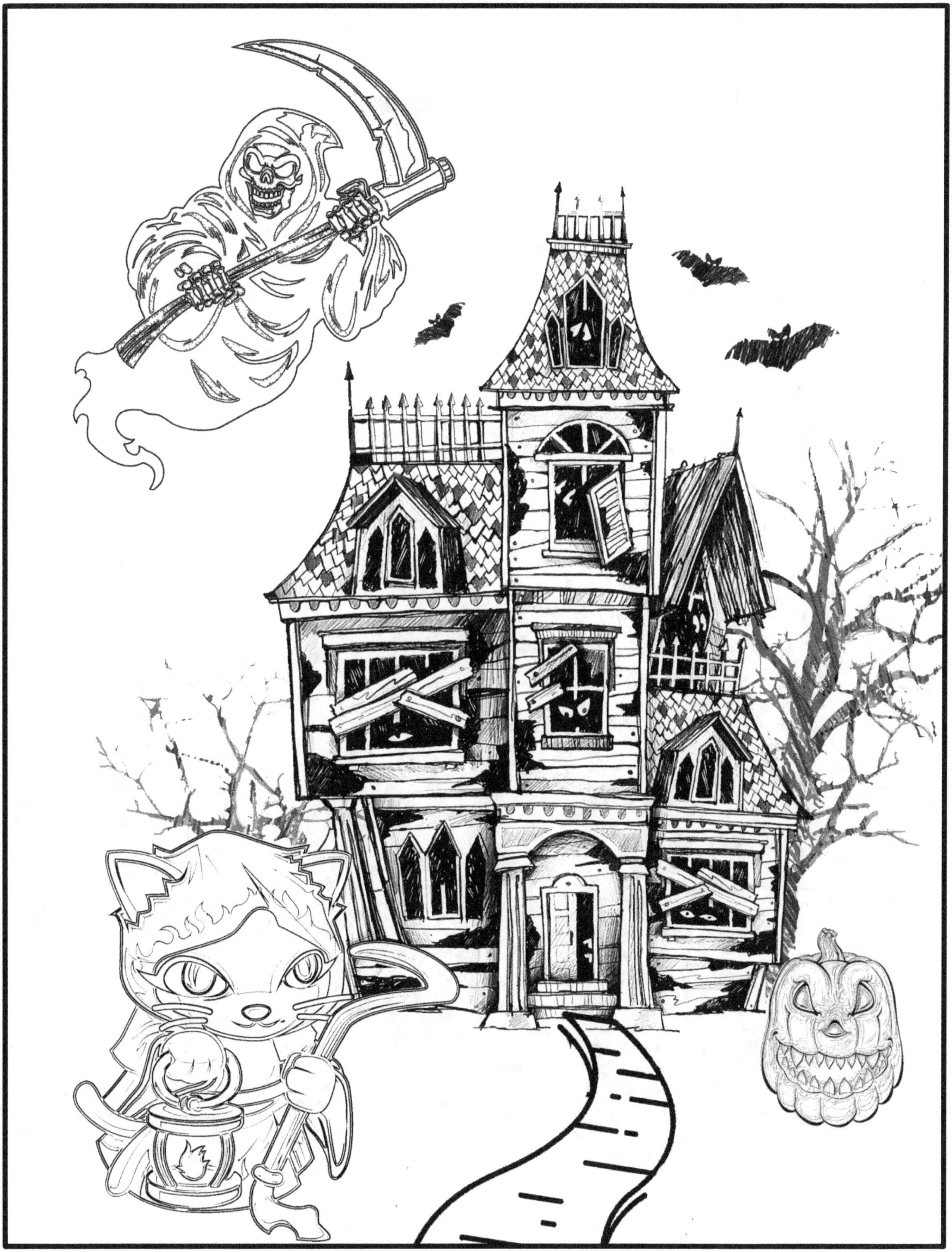

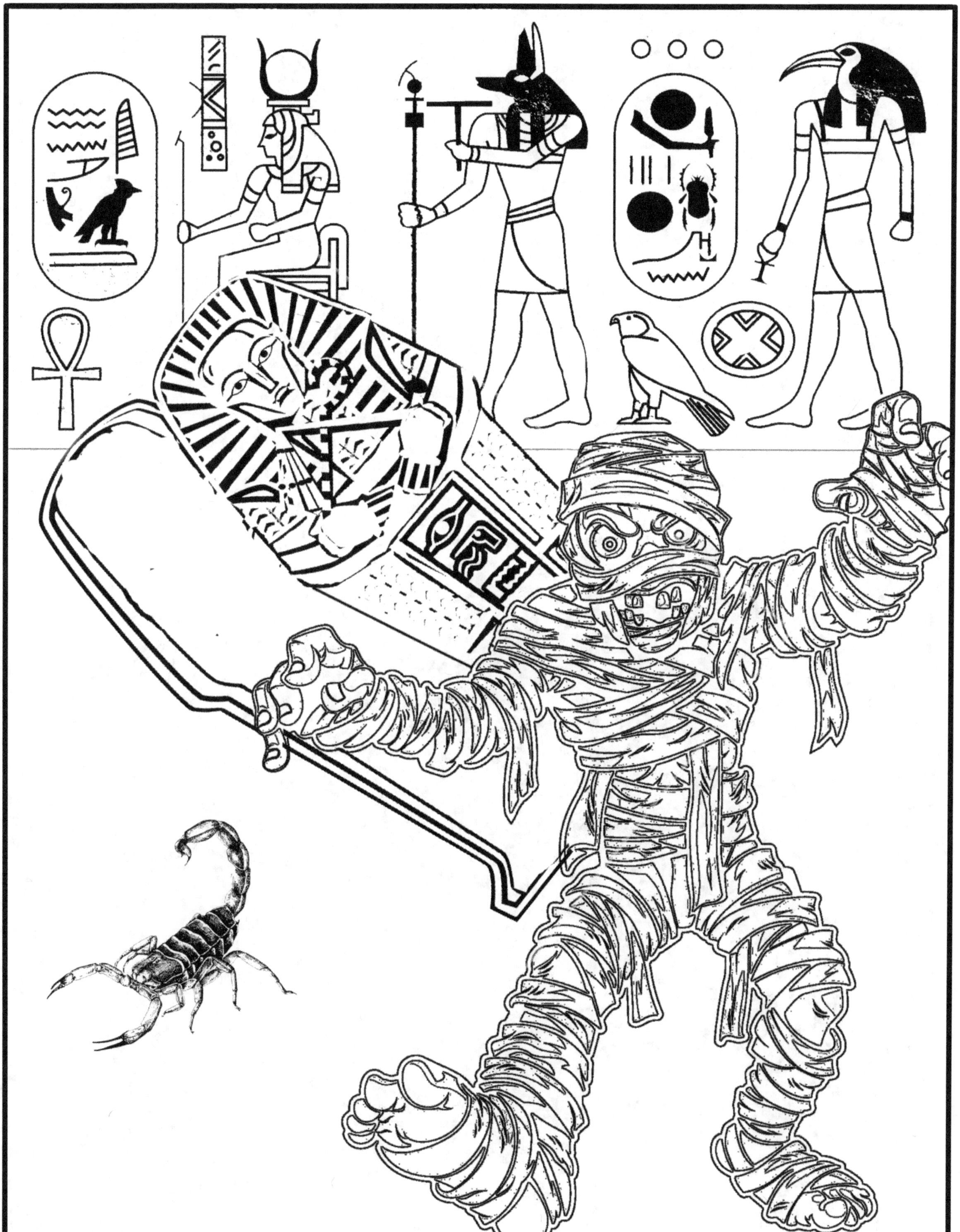

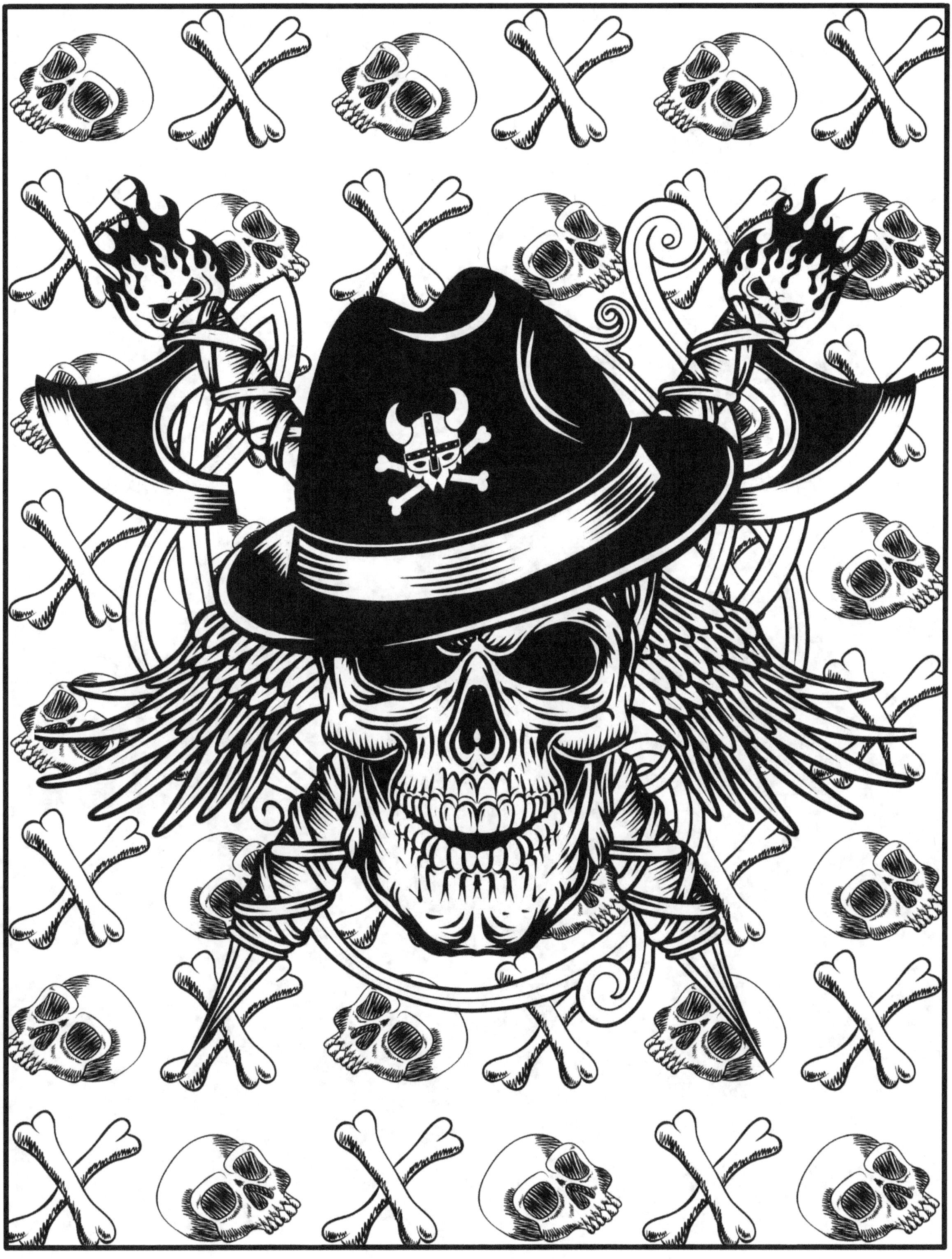

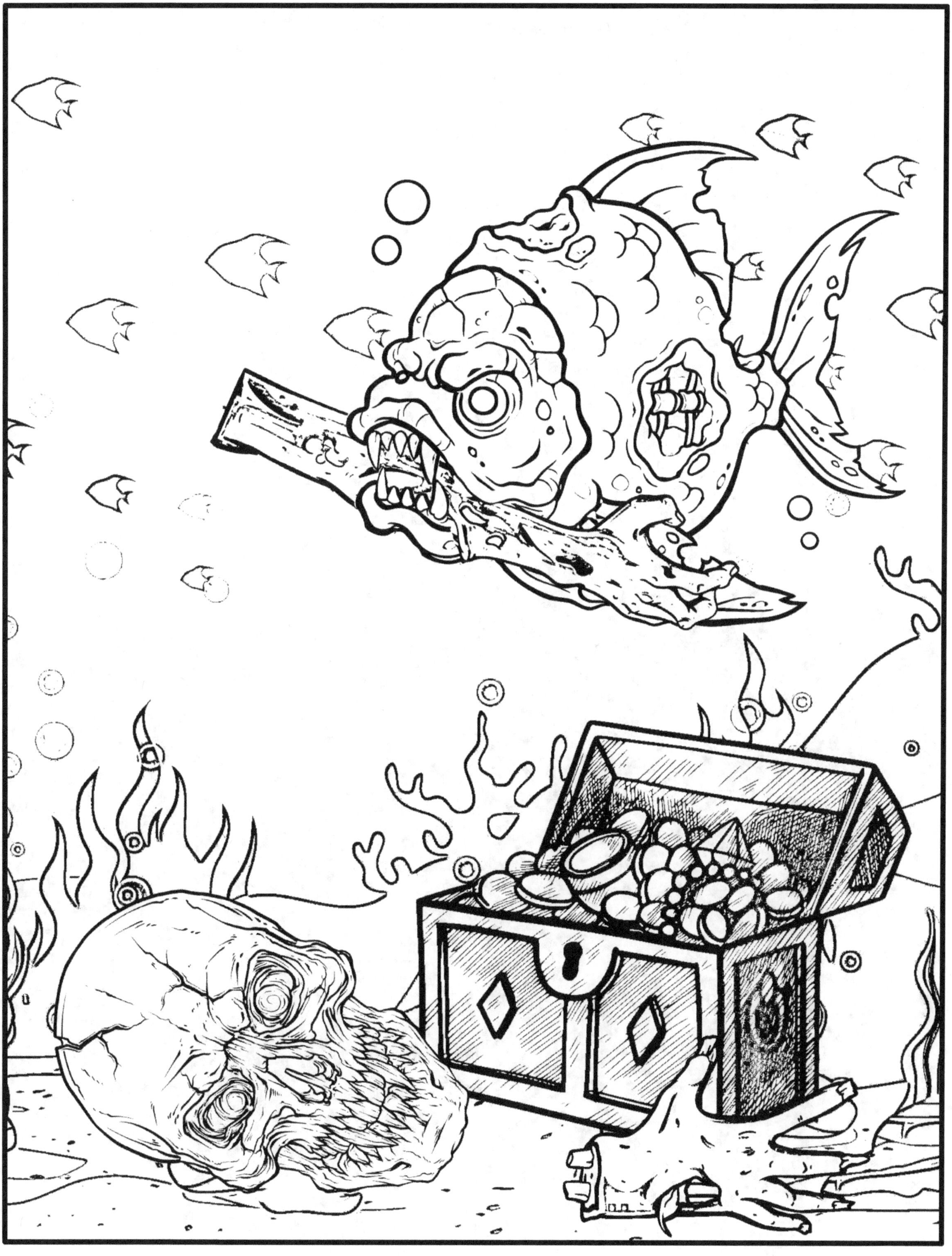

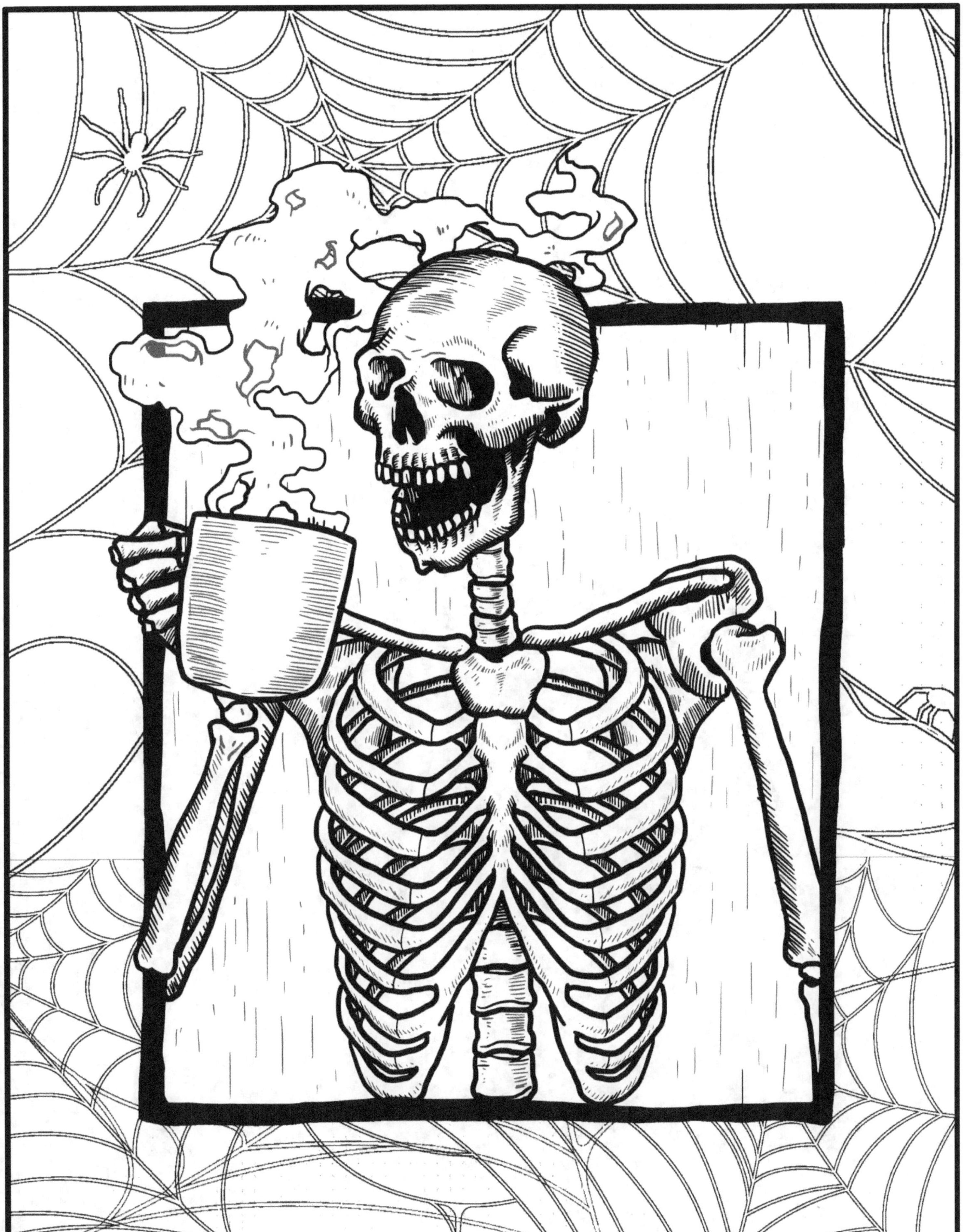

www.ingramcontent.com/pod-product-compliance
Lightning Source LLC
Chambersburg PA
CBHW081447220526
45466CB00008B/2544
*9781692611965*